Mantra

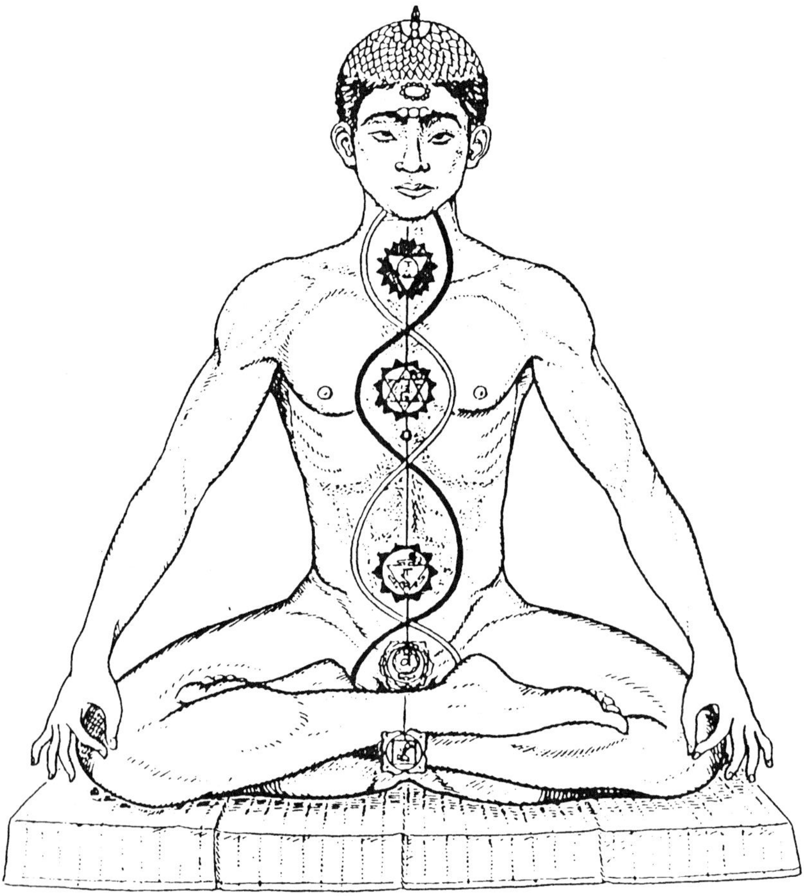

Mantra

Hearing the Divine in India and America

HAROLD G. COWARD
DAVID J. GOA

MOTILAL BANARSIDASS PUBLISHERS
PRIVATE LIMITED • DELHI

First Indian Edition : Delhi, 2008

ISBN: 978-81-208-3261-9

MOTILAL BANARSIDASS
41 U.A. Bungalow Road, Jawahar Nagar, Delhi 110 007
8 Mahalaxmi Chamber, 22 Bhulabhai Desai Road, Mumbai 400 026
203 Royapettah High Road, Mylapore, Chennai 600 004
236, 9th Main III Block, Jayanagar, Bangalore 560 011
Sanas Plaza, 1302 Baji Rao Road, Pune 411 002
8 Camac Street, Kolkata 700 017
Ashok Rajpath, Patna 800 004
Chowk, Varanasi 221 001

PRINTED IN INDIA
BY JAINENDRA PRAKASH JAIN AT SHRI JAINENDRA PRESS,
A-45 NARAINA, PHASE-I, NEW DELHI 110 028
AND PUBLISHED BY NARENDRA PRAKASH JAIN FOR
MOTILAL BANARSIDASS PUBLISHERS PRIVATE LIMITED,
BUNGALOW ROAD, DELHI 110 007

Contents

Preface

The original edition of this book was prompted by Diana L. Eck's *Darshan: Seeing the Divine in India.* That has proved to be a most effective book for introducing students to India and the way in which the divine is seen in Hindu religion. But darshan or seeing the being seen by the divine is only one-half of the Indian experience. The other half is hearing, and it is this dimension of the Hindu genius that has found its way into a number of other religions in India. Anyone who has traveled to India will recall the prominence of sound, from the din of car horns in the city to the loud chanting by devotees on the banks of the Ganges. Indeed, India is an experience of seeing *and* hearing. From the perspective of Indian religion, both senses provide powerful channels for the divine. As a complement to Diana Eck's *Darshan,* this book studies mantra as the hearing of the divine in India as it flowered in Hindu tradition, took root in Buddhism, Islam, and the Sikh tradition, and played a part in the restoration of contemplative prayer in Western Christianity.

Just as Westerners are often put off by the many strange shapes encountered in Indian religious images, so also they sometimes find the prayers, rituals, and chants that are constantly muttered to be a mystery. This study opens and tunes our modern Western ears so that we too can hear something of what the traditional Indian hears, can hear mantras and gain the beginning of an understanding of their nature and function.

It was the Hindu sensitivity to the power of the spoken word to transform consciousness that first drew us—rooted in the Christian tradition—to the study of Indian religious life. The Indian ability to hear the divine in sound, in the spoken words of scripture, in ritual and language in general, in the chanting of OM and the singing of hymns, is a continuing fascination.

The second edition of *Mantra: Hearing the Divine in India and North America* has given us the opportunity to expand our considerations, taking into account the remarkable ways mantra has come to be rooted in North American religious life over the last decade. This development has become so prominent that, as recently as August 4, 2003, *Time* magazine devoted its cover story to "The Science of Meditation," providing a popular map to the journey of mantra into the hearts and lives of millions. The genius of Indian religious experience and thinking is now a part of the religious life of North America, not only among the many Hindus, Buddhists, Sikhs, and Muslims who have come to make this continent their home but also for women and men who have come to the practice of mantra seeking a full and integrated life that affirms their dignity and their place in the cosmos.

Acknowledgments

We wish to acknowledge the encouragement of Harry Buck who, from the beginning, nourished the idea of this book and helped it to flower. Gerry Dyer and Cindy Atkinson of the Calgary Institute for the Humanities carefully typed the manuscript and deserve special thanks. Ronald Neufeldt, John Stocking, David Murray, and the Folklife Program of the Provincial Museum of Alberta were most generous in allowing their photographs to be used as illustrations. We appreciate the research assistance of Matthew Wangler, Matthew Francis, and Mickey Valle as well.

We gratefully acknowledge funding provided by the Department of Religious Studies, the Faculty of Humanities, the Institute for the Humanities and the vice president, Research, the University of Calgary.

We wish to thank Wendy Lochner of Columbia University Press for encouraging us to revise and expand the first edition of this book. We also thank Vicki Simmons and Linda Distad for their help in preparing the revised and expanded manuscript.

Mantra

I

Hearing the Sacred

SACRED SOUND IN INDIA

Stepping out of the airport in Mumbai, Delhi, or Calcutta, one is engulfed in a sea of sound. Taxis and motor scooters honk incessantly, and one is surrounded by a crush of people all speaking at the same time: "Taxi, Sir," "Hotel?" "Where do you want to go?" "Carry your case?" "Change money?"—and the small voice of the urchin in rags, "Please, sir, please," with cupped hands outstretched for a few coins. Indeed, part of the culture shock of India is its cacophony of sounds. Even nature joins into the general ruckus with the squawk of the ever present crows, the jabber of monkeys, and the early morning screech of India's national bird, the peacock.

One soon longs for quiet and finds it by rising before first light and venturing out into the awakening day. Imagine yourself stepping into a small side street of Banaras. The soft morning light is brightening to the East. All is quiet, and yet you begin to realize that around you the streets are full of activity. Forms of devout worshipers pass silently on their way to offer morning prayers and bathe in the Ganges. The merchants and traveling vendors with their distinctive cries of "Mangos," "Knives sharpened," or "Ice cream" have not yet appeared. But the morning quiet is broken by sounds of a different kind. From a second-floor window comes the sound of a morning prayer being chanted. As our ears become attuned to this muttered chant, we hear it rising from houses all around us as we wend our way through the narrow streets. The golden globe of the sun is just cresting the horizon as we reach the ghats or steps leading down from street level to the flowing water of the Ganges. The murmur of prayers being said around us steadily increases. A mumbled prayer is mixed with splashings of water from a man standing waist deep in the river. *Sadhus* or holy men, naked except for saffron loincloths, chant Sanskrit verses of the Veda, keeping count of their repetitions with prayer beads. Lay people join in with their own chants—all seem to be different and yet somehow blend together. A harmonious hymn of sound is raised to welcome the auspicious moment of the rising of the sun—the dawning of a new day.

As the sun ascends from the horizon and its first rays are felt warm upon one's skin, the chanted prayers increase in their intensity. To the Indian the light and warmth of the sun is a manifestation of the divine, but so is the sound of the morning chant that rises heavenward as an invocation of the new day. Speaking the Vedic chants and seeing the sunrise are both important experiences of the divine in India. Indeed, we can say that Indians specialize in seeing the divine in images of gods and goddesses and in hearing the divine in the sounds of daily life, from the morning prayer to the call of the crow, the screech of the ox cart axle or, in modern times, the incessant blaring of horns. In India all sound is perceived as being divine in origin, since it all arises from the one sacred source. Some sounds, however, are more powerful in evoking the divine within and around oneself than are others. Sound intrinsically bears the power of the sacred in India. In the Hindu hierarchy of scripture it is the Sruti, the heard text, which is preserved in oral tradition, that is the highest manifestation of the creative word. OM is the supreme example, since it is the divine seed sound from which all other sounds are said to arise. OṀ is, therefore, taken as the root mantra or sacred sound for the whole universe of sound.

The rising sun also signals the start of activity in the major temples of Banaras dedicated to the gods and goddesses of Hinduism. Within the imposing Vishvanath Temple, dedicated to Shiva, the priests begin to chant and dedicate offerings. Devotees crowd into the temple to have a view of the image of Shiva, a sight that is held to bring blessing, and to

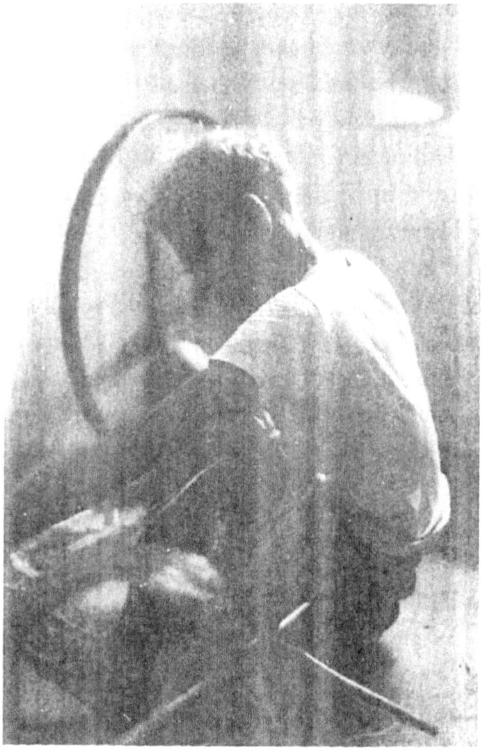

FIGURE 1.1 Throughout much of India common tasks such as spinning are done in public and private spaces. All contribute to the sounds of India. COURTESY JOHN STOCKING

watch the colorful ceremony. Throughout the day devotees stream to thousands of temples located all over Banaras to worship their favorite gods and goddesses. The variety of images from which they can choose reflects the richness through which the divine has revealed itself in the Hindu tradition: Vishnu, the heavenly king who descends to the world from time to time in various incarnations (*avataras*) to maintain cosmic stability; Shiva, the ascetic god who dwells in yogic meditation in the Himalayas generating energy that can be released into the world to refresh its vigor; Krishna, the manifestation of the divine as lover; Hanuman, the monkey god, who embodies strength, courage, and loyalty; Ganesha, the elephant-headed god who removes all obstacles for his followers; Durga, the warrior goddess who periodically defeats the forces of evil in order to protect the world; and Kali, the black mother goddess who dwells in cremation grounds and takes you to herself at death.

Dawn is a busy time at the cremation grounds on the banks of the Ganges River. Family funeral processions carry their stretcher-borne corpses down the steps to the spot where several funeral pyres are always burning. Pious Hindus believe that death near the Ganges or Banaras results in *moksa* or liberation from the endless cycles of birth, death, and rebirth—the ultimate spiritual goal of most Hindus. Banaras is also the home of many religious orders including a large number of ascetics or world renouncers. These holy men or women may be seen spending their day in meditation on the steps leading to the Ganges or at the cremation grounds. Their only possessions are a staff and a water pot. The males may be naked with long matted hair and bodies smeared with ash from the cremation grounds. The women may have shaved heads to show lack of concern for bodily appearance. All around them Hindu lay people are busily going about their daily tasks as merchants, businesspeople, tradespeople, artists, students, and professors from Banaras Hindu University, all busy with everyday family life. In their midst the ascetics look as if they are from another world, yet they are all part of the rich variety of lifestyles that Hindus may take on—one large extended family, as it were—full of diversity including many languages, cultures, and religious traditions, yet with an underlying sense of unity.

Hindus living in America cannot visit the Ganges at dawn, but many have a small pot of Ganges water on their home altar to help with morning prayers. Many of the same images (Vishnu, Ṣhiva, Durga, Krishna, Ganesha, and Kali) will be present on the home altar, which is often located in an upstairs bedroom dedicated as the worship room. There the family may gather or pray individually, using the same chanted prayers or mantras and the same repetitions of OM that are said in India. Hindu temples have been built in many American cities, providing places for family and the whole community to gather on ceremonial occasions. Cremation takes place in funeral homes rather than on the banks of the

Ganges. So, in many ways, the sacred practice of Hindus in Banaras goes on in modified form in America.

Just as the day begins with mantra chanting, so it also ends with an evening chant. At night, in India, the tropical birds join in with their "donc donc, donc donc." From the seashore comes the rhythmic roar of the waves. Not only is each day enclosed in sacred sound but so also is the whole of life. Indeed, it has been said, "From the mother's womb to the funeral pyre, a Hindu literally lives and dies in *mantra*."[1] This saying appears to express a truth that has dominated India for the past thousand years. For generations of post-Vedic Indians mantra is not primarily a Vedic text but rather the symbolic source of sacred sound that overflows textual boundaries until it encloses all of life—not only the speaking of humans but also of animals, particularly of birds. Mantra is also heard in the voices of fire, thunder, and rain.

Diana Eck has shown that India is filled with visual experiences of the divine—images in homes, temples, or roadside shrines—that a central act of worship "is to stand in the presence of the deity and to behold the image with one's own eyes, to see and be seen by the deity."[2] That is now also happening in Hindu diaspora communities all over North America where temples have been built and images installed.[3] But India is also permeated by sonic experiences of the divine. Drums, bells, gongs, cymbals, conches, flutes, and a wide variety of vocalizations are often heard, sometimes simultaneously, invoking and evoking the divine within temple, home, or sacred space. As suggested above, the first impression to the outsider may be one of chaos and cacophony, an ensemble of "noise" with no apparent rhyme or reason. But, if we empathize with the presuppositions of the Indian culture and religious traditions, we come to realize that there is an underlying religious foundation for the experience of sound in general and for the saying of specific mantras (words or sounds) in particular. Indeed we could parallel Diana Eck's statement about the visual experience of the divine by saying that in India the central act of worship is hearing the mantra or sacred sound with one's own ears and chanting the mantra with one's voice.

Hearing and saying the mantra is an act of worship that "tunes" one to the basic sound or vibration of the universe. By a continual hearing and chanting, one purifies and transforms one's life until it vibrates in harmony with the divine, which is itself pure sound. Indeed, we find Indian religion filled with many different versions of "sonic theology." For Hindu India, then, *the act of worship* involves both a seeing and being seen by the divine image *(darshan)* and also hearing and speaking the divine sound *(mantra)*. Both are present and central to the worship of most lay people in India. For some more advanced worshipers the sound may totally displace the image so that the concentration is on the sound alone. In this book our focus will be on mantra, the hearing and speaking aspect of experiencing the divine in India and America.

It has been said that there is no parallel to the concept of darshan, of seeing and being seen by the divine in the Western religions.[4] As Diana Eck puts it, when the gaze of the huge eyes of the image of Lord Krishna meets those of the worshiper standing on tiptoe in the crowd, there is a special exchange of vision that is itself a form of "touching," of intimate knowing. Such an exchange of vision is darshan and is fundamental to Hindu worship. So also the practice of hearing and speaking the mantra is an act in which the consciousness of the individual may experience a tuning into the divine sound of the cosmos. This is what Agehananda Bharati means when he says "*mantra is* not meaningful in any descriptive or even persuasive sense, but within the mystical universe of discourse."[5] Mantra chanting is verified not by what it describes or cognitively reveals but by the complex vibration or feeling tone it creates in the practicing person.

Is there a parallel to the Indian practice of mantra, of hearing and being heard by the divine in the West? When one considers a religious practice from outside, that practice may acquire a charm and authority out of its very foreignness and become imbued with a power that comes from partial misunderstanding or incomprehension. Often, for the religiously inquisitive sons and daughters of Western religious traditions, this is fed by ignorance of similar aspects of religious sensibility and discipline within their own traditions and in popular culture. For example, there are the chants we experienced as children in learning times tables by repeating them as a class, the special sayings chanted while skipping, or the chants used to cheer on our school team. If we grew up in a Christian context we may have learned to chant the Hail Mary, the Lord's Prayer, or the

Twenty-third Psalm. Throughout the book we will refer to such Western examples in order to sharpen the reader's understanding of the hearing and speaking of the divine and ultimately of mantra.

Certainly in the great faiths of the West, Judaism, Christianity, and Islam, the divine word is spoken and heard in ways that are profoundly sacred. In the biblical creation narrative, cosmos and all creatures come into being at God's word. God speaks the creation into being. The Gospel of John, long a favorite text for many Christians, opens with the words, "In the beginning was the Word, and the Word was with God and the Word was God" (John 1:1).

Muslims, as well, have a sense of the sacredness of the word. The Qur'an is understood as the very words of God, recorded faithfully by the Prophet Muhammad as dictated by the angel Gabriel. Anyone who has witnessed Muslims chanting the Qur'an will have been touched by the power of the divine word. Throughout much of the Muslim world the faithful sit with the Qur'an open, chanting page after page in meditative prayer. Many of these people are illiterate; the divine word has been committed to memory through years of recitation. They use the book as a kind of prop, but the tradition has taken form orally and is practiced in acts of meditation and oral prayer. The word of God is always heard and chanted in meditative prayer.

Often in our study of the religious traditions of the West we have limited our exploration to the historical, textual, and philosophical forms faith takes. When we examine the liturgical life, however, we find ourselves on ground that may have a good deal more in common with the great traditions of India than we have previously assumed.

When we consider Eastern Orthodox Christians praying the words of scripture in the Divine Liturgy, or the monks of that tradition praying the Jesus Prayer while kneading bread or doing any of the other common tasks of daily life, or Roman Catholic faithful saying the rosary or the Common of the Mass, or the rich and pious hymnology of Protestants, we begin to see the power of the sacred word at work, expressing the longing of the human heart and the joy of communion with the divine. Word, sacred word, is clearly central for the religious traditions of the West as well. But is it mantra? This is a question we will address throughout the book. Now, however, let us turn to a more systematic introduction to mantra in the sacred sound of India.

MANTRA IN THE SACRED SOUND OF INDIA

India is not merely, or even principally, the land of Vedanta. It is the land of mantra. To know and to love Indian religious life means coming to terms with mantric utterance.

—Harvey Alper, *Understanding Mantras*

Before coming to mantra itself, four basic ideas of Indian thought need to be introduced briefly: *anadi*, *karma*, *samsara*, and *moksa*. They provide the basic context for the functioning of sacred sound in India. *Anadi* is the notion that the universe is beginningless—everything has been going on beginninglessly. This includes the sacred sounds of the mantras, which are held to be beginningless, uncreated, and eternal. Of course, there are cycles of creation, with each cycle going through the stages of sprouting, growing, maturing, and dying, but leaving behind a seed-form out of which the next cycle may arise. The image is an agricultural one of a seed sprouting, maturing, blossoming, withering, and perishing, yet dropping off a seed out of which the cycle may arise again. The difficult aspect to grasp, from the Western perspective, is that there is no first cycle. These cycles of the universe have been going on beginninglessly. And at the start of each cycle, say the orthodox Hindus, the sacred mantras of the Hindu Veda are spoken forth as an important part of the creating process itself as well as a revelation of divine truth.

Karma is a word that is now fairly common in the West but often little understood. There are many definitions of karma in the Indian tradition, some making karma appear quite deterministic. One of the clearest descriptions, however, is found in the *Yoga Sutras of Patanjali*.[6] This concept is widely influential and has the added advantage of making room for free will. It runs as follows. Every time you do an action or think a thought a memory trace or karmic seed is laid down in the storehouse of your unconscious. There it sits waiting for circumstances conducive to it

FIGURE 1.2 A Hindu priest in Canada, Sushil Kalia, chants mantra as he elevates the offering of light. COURTESY DAVID J. GOA

sprouting forth as an impulse, instinct, or predisposition to do the same action or think the same thought again. Notice that the karmic impulse from the unconscious does not cause anything, it is not mechanistic in nature. Rather it simply *predisposes* you to do an action or think a thought. Room is left for the function of free will. Through the use of your free choice you decide either to go along with the karmic impulse, in which case it is reinforced and strengthened, or to say "no" and negate it, in which case its strength diminishes until it is finally removed from the unconscious. Karmas can be either good or bad. Good actions and thoughts lay down good karmic traces in the unconscious for the predisposing of future good karmic impulses. Evil actions and thoughts do the reverse. Scripture and tradition taken together distinguish between good and evil.

How does all of this apply to mantras? Speaking or thinking a mantra is an action that lays down a karmic trace in the unconscious. Chanting a mantra over and over reinforces that karmic trace (*samskara*) until a deep root or habit pattern (*vasana*) is established. Correctly chanting a good mantra, such as OM or a verse of Vedic scripture, reinforces good karma and removes negative karmas or impulses by preventing their blossoming or maturing so that they wither away, leaving no trace behind. In this way mantra chanting can be seen to be a powerful psychological tool for purifying and transforming consciousness.

According to karma theory, then, all the impulses you are experiencing at this moment result from actions and thoughts done in this life. But what if you experience an impulse, either good or evil, that seems completely out of character with the way you have lived since birth? That karmic impulse arises from an action or thought you did in a previous life—which introduces the third basic idea, namely, *samsara* or rebirth. Your unconscious contains not only all the karmic traces from actions and thoughts done in this life but also in the life before this and so on, backward infinitely since there is no absolute beginning. In reality, then, your unconscious is like a huge granary full of karmic seeds or memory traces that are constantly sprouting up, as conducive situations arise, impelling you toward good or evil actions or thoughts. No wonder we constantly feel ourselves being pulled and pushed by our karmic desires. But the possibility of free choice always allows us to take control over these impulses, and mantra chanting gives us a powerful psychological and spiritual tool to use in directing this process.

Samsara provides us with the idea of a ladder of rebirth. At the bottom are the animals, in the middle the humans, and at the top the gods.

Assume that you are a human being. If in this life you use your free choice to act on the good karmic impulses and negate the evil ones, then at the end of this life you will have increased the number of good *karmas* and decreased the number of evil karmas in your unconscious. At death (where the karmas function like coins in a banker's balance) the increase

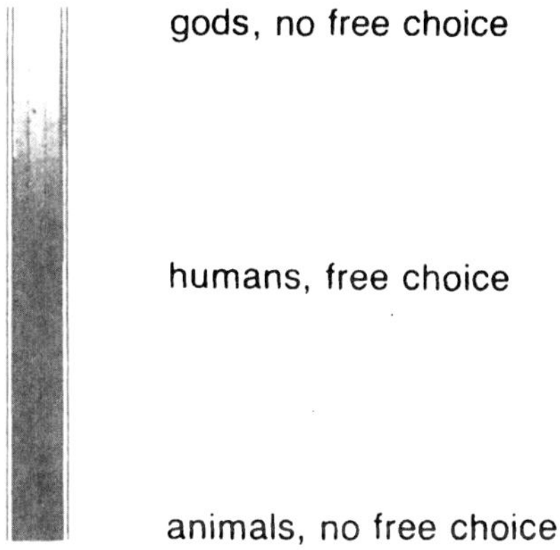

FIGURE 1.3

in good karmas will automatically cause you to be reborn further up the ladder. If you repeat the same procedure of acting on the good and negating the evil over many lifetimes you will gradually spiral toward the top of the ladder and be reborn in the realm of the gods. Unlike humans, gods have no free choice, no power to act. All you can do is to enjoy the honor of being a god—of sitting in the mayor's chair for a day, as it were—until the merit built up from your good choices over countless lives is used up and you are reborn a human at the top of the human scale with the prospect of continued birth, death, and rebirth to look forward to. But what if in this life you used your free choice to go the opposite way—to act on the evil karmic impulses and to negate the good? Then at death you would have increased the number of bad karmas, reduced the number of good karmas, and automatically been reborn a step lower down the ladder. And if this negative pattern was repeated through many lifetimes you would spiral down and eventually be reborn as an animal. Animals are simply human beings in a different karmic form (which logically explains the Indian practice of vegetarianism—to eat an animal is to engage in cannibalism). Unlike humans, animals have no free choice. Their fate is to endure the sufferings that their instincts cause them. When they have suffered sufficiently to expiate or purge off the bad karma they built up through many lifetimes of making evil choices, they are then reborn as human beings with free choice and a chance to move up the ladder again through the process of birth, death, and rebirth.

When one thinks of this process as having been going on beginninglessly and sees the prospect of being born, growing old, dying, and being reborn apparently endlessly, the question comes to mind, "How can I get release (moksa)?" Hinduism gives one answer, Buddhism gives a different answer. Yet in both answers mantra chanting is featured as a powerful means of obtaining release.

In Hinduism the thing that causes one to be reborn is the karma within one's own consciousness. The chanting of mantras is one of the most powerful practices for the purging of karmas, and when the last karma is removed, moksa is realized. Although conceptualized differently by different Hindu schools, moksa may generally be thought of as the removal of karmas that make us appear to be separate from Brahman (the divine). When the last veiling or obstructing karma is removed, the fact that one is, and has always been, nothing but Brahman is revealed. That is moksa—the direct realization of one's own oneness with the divine.

The concept of mantra as powerful sacred sound is associated with one of India's ancient scriptures, the Rgveda.[7] India shares with the rest of the world a fascination with what Rudolf Otto has called numinous sounds,[8] sounds that go beyond the rational and the ethical to evoke a direct face-to-face contact with the holy. Otto conceived of the numinous with a typically Western emphasis on the experience of the distance, the separation, between human beings and God. For Hindus in the Rgvedic context the cosmos is peopled by gods sometimes thought of in personal ways. For example, prayers or mantras are spoken to gods such as Varuna to maintain relationships with them so that they will act for the devotee. However, the Rgveda also saw mantras as the means by which the power of truth and order that is at the very center of the Vedic universe could be evoked. That truth, however, is not thought of as a personal God, like Yahweh or Allah, but as the impersonal rta or divine order of reality. In his classic article, "The Indian *Mantra*," Gonda points out that mantras are not thought of as products of discursive thought, human wisdom, or poetic fantasy "but as flash-lights of the eternal truth, seen by those eminent men who have come into supersensuous contact with the Unseen."[9] Sri Aurobindo puts it even more vividly, "The language of the *Veda* is itself a *sruti*, a rhythm not composed by the intellect but heard, a divine Word that came vibrating out of the Infinite to the inner audience of the man who had previously made himself fit for the impersonal knowledge."[10] The Vedic seers supersensuously "heard" these divine mantras not as personal but as divinely rooted words and spoke them in the Hindu scripture or Veda as an aid to those less spiritually advanced. By concentrating one's mind upon such a mantra, the devotee invokes the power and truth inherent in the seers' divine intuition and so purifies his or her consciousness. It is this understanding that is behind the long-standing Indian practice of the repeated chanting of mantras as a means for removing karmic ignorance or impurity from one's personality. The more difficulties to be overcome, the more repetitions are needed. The deeper is one's separation from the Eternal Absolute, the more one must invoke the mantra. Contrary to what our modern minds quickly tend to assume, the Hindu chanting a mantra in morning and evening worship is not simply engaging in an empty superstition. From the Indian perspective such chanted words have power to confirm and increase truth and order (*rta*) within one's character and in the wider universe. Chanting a Vedic mantra has a spiritually therapeutic effect upon the devotee and a cosmic significance as well. Hindus maintain that the holiness of the mantra or divine word is intrinsic, that one participates in it not by discursive understanding but by hearing and reciting it.[11] Vedic mantras can be single words, sentences, or complete verses.

During the Rgvedic period the notion of mantra comes to focus more on the language of ritual and less on the poetic insight born of the face-to-face contemplation of rta or divine order. A new view of ritual speech arises. The creatively eloquent insight of the Vedic seer is transformed into a known formula that will function effectively in a ritual context.[12] For the Rgvedic poets, mantras have power, and the source of that power is the truth and order (rta) that stands at the very center of the universe.

The power encapsulated in a mantra is released when it is spoken. As Hacker put it, mantras when spoken are capable of bringing about a reality not only at the psychological level but even in the material order of things.[13] Therefore, the speaker of the mantra must realize that he or she is handling power; power that can be used for good or for ill. In Hebrew thought as well the notion that spoken words have power is present (see Exodus 20:7). Speaking the mantra can have a purifying effect upon the speaker and the universe or, if spoken in malice or ignorance, the power unleashed can be harmful to the individual and to the universe. In this sense mantra as sacred word can bless or curse. It is powerful.

Such holy power should not be treated lightly, and so supervision of the ritual chanting of mantras was a responsibility given to the priests of India. Indeed, mantras are thought to be so highly charged that unless properly handled by a priest or by a person under the close supervision of a priest, the mantra can fall back upon and burn its speaker. The Vedic mantra is like a high voltage channel that puts its speaker in direct connection with the power source of the universe. And that power source is rta, the transcendent truth of the cosmic and human orders. It is the power of that truth that is released when the mantra is spoken and then repeated over and over.

Chanting the mantra fills one's consciousness with the power of truth and fosters the dominance of truth over chaos in the surrounding universe. Through the truth power of the mantra one attunes oneself to the cosmic order (rta) of the universe. One is placed in the midst of revelation of ultimate truth. For the Rgveda, revelation is not a matter of God intervening in the affairs of the world, rather, it is the insight that naturally arises through the chanting of the mantras truly formulated by the ancient *rsis* or seers. The rsis themselves directly experienced the ultimate truth, meditated upon it in their hearts, and carefully expressed it in well-formed mantras. "*Mantras* formulated in the heart are true not just because they capture the truth of some cosmological occurrence but because they themselves have participated, and continue to participate, in the same cosmological events."[14] Mantras not only articulate truth, they are the truth. They have participated in the primordial revelation of truth by the

FIGURE 1.4 Morning ablutions and meditations at the Vankataswar temple near Madras. COURTESY RONALD NEUFELDT

Vedic rsis, and through their repetition they become the means by which the cosmic truth and order is manifest and preserved.

The devotee sitting on the banks of the Ganges at dawn and chanting the Agni mantra aids in the daily retrieval of the sun out of darkness and reestablishes the light of truth at the center of his or her consciousness for the coming day. Agni is the god of fire, light, and truth. As dawn becomes visible to humans on earth, the contemplation of Agni links the worshiper to the mystery of the recurrence of the sun each morning, to the light and truth at the center of the cosmos. The following Rgvedic hymn describes Agni's relationship to speech that is well formed, insightful, and therefore powerful as mantra.

Your delightful countenance, mighty Agni, shines out
next to the [daytime] sun. Bright to look at, it is also
seen at night.
On your body, there is glossy food [i.e., butter] to see.
You, Agni, with eloquent tongue
god-serving mortals seek out as the first god, immortal!
to win with prayers him who wards off hostility,
the domestic, insightful lord of the home.
Dull-mindedness is far from us, far away anxiety
far away all injurious thought, whenever you watch over us.
By night, Agni son of strength, you are auspicious to
the one you accompany for well being, god![15]

This hymn is significant for two reasons. First, it locates Agni as the vital energy at the mysterious center of the cosmos. It is from Agni that all insight, all revelation comes. Humans would not be able to think, imagine, speak or sing without the words bestowed by Agni. Second, it is these words, as a gift of grace from Agni, that the inspired poet or rsis can turn into mantras with power for ritual use.[16]

The development of the priestly class in the later Rgvedic and Brahmanic periods focuses on the question of how to use this power that the mantra possesses for good. The answer reached is clear. To make the mantra work one must pronounce it. As the Rgveda puts it,

If these mantras of ours remain unspoken they will bring
no joy, even on the most distant day.[17]

Pronouncing the mantra correctly in its proper ritual context releases its power. For this to happen, the supervision of a priest is seen as essential. Under the guidance of a priest, the Rgvedic mantra is an instrument of power to produce results both personal and cosmic. Mantras spoken in ritual activity actually do something. Thus, even from their earliest conception in the Rgveda, mantras are classical examples of what are now called "speech acts."[18] However, whereas modern thought emphasizes the performative nature of the speech act at the expense of its communication function, the Rgvedic seers are emphatic that while the spoken mantra can do things; the basis for that power is located in its revelation of truth (*ta, satya*). Although mantras from later Indian tradition can be of a non-sensical nature,[19] in the Rgvedic period it seems clear that a mantra must reveal meaning. Indeed the original sense of mantra as a vehicle for reflection and revelation becomes operationalized by the late Rgvedic seers and priests. "*Mantra* is the tool, the mechanism, for yoking the reflective powers of the seer into the machinery of ritual."[20]

As the use of mantra goes through later developments, one or the other of this double aspect receives elaboration. On the one hand, the mantra becomes a key to meditation, to the establishment and maintenance of divine accessibility. On the other, mantra chanting becomes merely an instrumental power to achieve worldly ends (e.g., getting sons) with little attention paid to the aspect of divine revelation. Indeed, there are many people who treat mantra in this quasi-magical fashion. Even in these cases, however, we must remember that for many of the faithful of India—Hindu, Buddhist, and Sikh—being a householder and a parent are simply stages in the inestimably long journey to a fully spiritual existence. Therefore, seeking in a quite vulgar way the material blessings associated with these stages is part of that ultimate journey. As the seer is transformed from a poet-saint who meditates and makes his life an empty channel to the divine to a priest who knows how to make the ritual effective, the performative function of mantras is given more emphasis. Consequently there is a stress on proper pronunciation in the correct ritual context for the desired result to be achieved. These are indeed the issues that become central in the Brahmanas, the prose ritual commentaries that are added to the earlier collections of Vedic hymns. But the other aspect of mantra, its revelation function, is not lost. Indeed the Vedic poet's wish that the mantra be both powerful and have an inspired meaning is nicely expressed: "May we pronounce that mantra well that was fashioned for him from the heart; he will understand it to be sure (Rgveda 2.35.2ab)."[21]

With the Upanisads—a second level of prose commentaries on the Vedic hymns—the pendulum swings away from the emphasis on ritual and back to mantra as the means to revealed knowledge. Instead of the ritual priest it is the guru or teacher in the context of student-teacher dialogue who skillfully uses the mantras. The result desired now, however, is not material wealth or sons but release (moksa) from the beginningless and seemingly endless cycle of birth-death-rebirth (karma-samsara). When enough of the obscuring karma or ignorance has been removed by the dialogues with the guru and individual meditation, the teacher's speaking of mantras such as *tat tvam asi* ("that thou art") evokes a flash of insight revealing the unity of the individual devotee with the cosmic reality now called Brahman. When at the right moment the guru speaks "tat tvam asi" to the student, an awakening so powerful as to remove all remaining karma dawns upon the mind and grows into an insight so brilliant and all-embracing that the unity of all things in Brahman is directly realized. This, for the Hindu, is the redemptive moment of final release that, in the Upanisads, is effected only by mantra-induced knowledge. Later traditions such as the Yogic, Mimamsa, Grammarian, and Vedanta schools give further development to the initial insight of the Vedas.

Some medieval yoga traditions take the *nada* or sound vibrations themselves to be the basis for meditational techniques aimed at the realization of release (moksa). The Gorakhnath (or Nath) tradition specialized in the use of sacred sound as a yoga in itself.[22] Thus, the original mantra experience of the Vedic seers, mantra as a means to realize the truth of ultimate reality, is given systematic elaboration.

Such redemptive uses of mantras as a means to realize ultimate reality in this life are, however, very much in the minority in India. Within Hinduism most mantras are employed for ritual purposes to seek immediate benefit or to purify and nurture an individual's journey toward ultimate reality, which will continue over many lifetimes. Whether employed in worship (*puja*) or in the ritual acts of daily Hindu life, mantra use is mainly for the achieving of benefits in this life or the next and not for final release (moksa). In all such cases the ritual action is either accompanied by mantras or consists simply of their utterance. In the structure of virtually all the samskaras, sacraments that accompany a new stage in life for the individual, mantra is central. Characteristically, these mantras evoke the benefits of life progeny, prosperity, and longevity, for they initiate and speak of the journey to liberation, the ultimate goal of moksa. This can be clearly seen in the Vedic initiation, the *Upanayana samskara.*[23]

The Upanayana samskara plays a pivotal role in the Hindu understanding of the four stages of life: student, householder, forest dweller, holy wanderer. These four *asramas*, as they are called, provide a framework for the religious, psychological, and social needs of the individual from childhood to old age. Each stage, ideally a twenty-five-year span, has its appropriate commitments and disciplines. Each span properly lived out will serve the human community through ethical fidelity and nurture the soul along the path leading to ultimate liberation.

The first stage is a period of celibacy and learning, of nurturing physical development, mental and spiritual health, strength and endurance. It is the *Brahmacarya* asrama, the student life, hinged, as its title suggests, on mastering the basic religious rituals and texts (learned by heart). There is no sexual activity at this stage, as all one's energy is directed to study.

The second stage, *Grhastha* asrama, sees the individual take up all the duties, responsibilities, and opportunities of a householder including getting a job, marrying, having children, and fulfilling community responsibilities. *Artha*, the pursuit of wealth, *kama*, the pursuit of legitimate desires, and *dharma*, the doing of religious and moral duties are all appropriate goals for the householder stage of life.

When the primary responsibility of raising children has been properly discharged, the householder is freed from immediate needs and interests of his family. When hair turns grey, skin wrinkles, and grandchildren arrive he may retire into the forest, the *Vanaprastha* asrama, with his wife. There they devote themselves to spiritual study and discipline under the guidance of a guru. While husband and wife may remain together, their relationship is purely Platonic, with no sexual activity—that is appropriate only to the householder stage.

The final stage of life is characterized by complete surrender, *Mahaprasthana*, the life of the recluse or holy wanderer. This period of life is devoted—with the support of the community—to meditation on the Word of God and the practice of meditation. No longer is there special attachment to husband, wife, or children. It is not that affection for these is lessened or lost, but that all others are raised to that same level in one's love. All women are seen as one's mother, wife, or sister; all men as one's father, husband, or brother. As a holy wanderer (*sannyasin*) one is completely freed from restrictions of family, caste, and village loyalties and instead is universally committed to love, teach, and help whomever one meets on life's path. In short, one has become a guru. As with the forest dweller, there is no sexual activity at this stage. It is at this stage of life that the goal of final release from rebirth (moksa) is sought.

Entrance into spiritual life begins with the Upanayana. The Upanayana is regarded as a second birth. The young student *brahmacarin* will be initiated through mantra, will be taught mantra, and will speak mantra, all in the hope that eventually he will hear mantra in a liberating way. He leaves his mother and goes to the household of the one who will teach him the Vedas, who will teach him the mantras, who will teach him as his first guru that his soul, *jiva*, is to be one with God. In the early Vedic period girls as well as boys received initiation. The brahmacarin is identified with the forest dwellers, who through complete surrender devoted themselves to the Word of God and to the hearing of the mantra. This identification is symbolized by the garment given to the boy, a cloth representing the deerskin worn by the forest dwellers, and by the threads of deerskin attached to the sacred thread that is placed over his shoulder. (The Upanayana is often called the sacred thread ceremony.) When the student has the thread placed around him he is reminded that he is to attain the spiritual illumination of the rsis.

After he has been wrapped in the cloth, and before the sacred thread is placed over his shoulder, the brahmacarin is identified with the Vedas. A girdle is tied around his waist by the teacher with the words, "A youth well attired, dressed, come hither. He, being born, becomes glorious. Wise sages extol him, devout ones, turn their minds to god."[24] The triple cord design of the girdle is symbolic of the three Vedas. The student is wrapped in mantra, wrapped in scripture, wrapped in the garments of those who sought the divine with singleness of heart.

Now the boy is prepared for the initiation. The waters used for purification are consecrated through mantra. Following the purification, the Gayatri Mantra can be invoked for the first time. This mantra will be said by every initiated man in the morning and evening throughout his life. The teacher reaches over the right shoulder and touching the heart of the

FIGURE 1.5 The Upanayana initiation of a young boy. His father is offering ghee to Agni, the god of fire. The priest presides over the ritual. COURTESY RONALD NEUFELDT

student says, "Into my will I take thy heart. Thy mind shall follow my mind. In my word thou shalt rejoice with all thy heart. Thy mind shall follow my mind. In my word thou shalt rejoice with all thy heart. May Brhaspati join thee and me."[25] All significant insight and learning come out of a deep harmony between the teacher and student. Genuine progress on the path of illumination comes when the guru, touching the very soul of the initiate through the mantra, brings about the union of this particular soul with the divine.

After the student is told that his teachers are Indra, Agni, and the *acarya*, he is ready to receive the Savitri Mantra, the apex of the initiation. The teacher looks directly into his face and recites: "Let us meditate on the most excellent light of the Creator (the sun); May he guide our intellect." This rather lengthy mantra is recited slowly in a memorable meter so the student can begin to retain it. This marks the second birth of the boy. The teacher is his father, and Savitri—the goddess personifying the Gayatri Mantra, wife of Brahman and mother of the four Vedas—is the mother of the student in his second birth.

Once the Gayatri Mantra is learned, the twice-born with his teacher can rekindle the sacred fire and offer the ritual sacrifice, which is all mantra. The student is no longer a child and has taken the first conscious steps on the long journey to liberation. From now on he is encouraged to serve the acarya by drawing water, collecting fuel for the sacrifice, and by keeping silence. These, of course, are not about simple servitude but carry with them symbolic meaning: to draw on the ambrosia of revelation, kindle the fire of illumination, and to do it all with unquestioning vigor. Harmony with the teacher, the guru, is essential, and all the gods and goddesses are invoked to assist the student to live up to the full range of responsibilities in life. If he does so he will have taken another step in the journey to liberation.

As with the student in the Upanayana ceremony, so it is with householders in their daily life. The householder, under the supervision of a priest, utters words that will produce a result, even though that result may not be visible. Yet the person may well be convinced that such mantras drive away demons causing bodily or mental illness, transform water into nectar, or provide protection from evil spells. Does the intention or sincerity of the devotee matter in such mantra use? When the mantra is aimed at spiritual release (moksa), the answer is clearly "yes." But in the case of obligatory rites or the everyday rituals commonly practiced, the only necessary condition for such mantras to produce the desired result is that they be used according to the strictly prescribed rules.[26] It is, of course, the job of the priest to ensure that the rules are followed, that the mantras are correct and correctly pronounced, thereby ensuring an efficacious result. For this service it is appropriate that the priest be paid a suitable fee. This detail is omitted or trifled with at one's peril. Priests, it is said, can perform the mantras in such a way that their results will backfire upon the devotee if the fee paid was inadequate.

Mantras also frequently accompany daily acts other than those of worship, for example, baths, meals, work, laying a cornerstone, and so on. Structuring the whole day, with each act entered, accompanied by and concluded with mantra, is illustrated in *The Daily Practice of the Hindus*,[27] a manual giving all the mantras (close to two hundred pages worth) used in daily life among the Sama-Vedi Brahmanas in Bengal and the Yajur-Vedis in North India. It divides the day into eight parts of three hours each, called *yama*. The day begins with waking at 4:30 A.M., washing and ablutions, sipping water, cleansing one's teeth, bathing and meditation. All of these acts, the obvious religious ones and the caring for the body, are done with accompanying mantra chanting.

This is the pattern for the unfolding of the day. Whether it is working for the family's maintenance, the study of sacred or secular literature, meals, visiting with friends and family, or the final conversation between the spouses before bed, each act is sanctified with mantras. They help the person doing the action to focus upon the sacred meaning of the action. Pushed to its limit this approach of sanctifying ordinary everyday actions can reach the point where every action, including every breath, is accompanied by a mantra. For example, the Hare Krishnas, commonly seen on North American streets in the 1970s and still active in America today, strive to say their mantra to Lord Krishna with every breath:

Hare Krishna, Hare Krishna
Krishna Krishna, Hare Hare
Hare Rama, Hare Rama
Rama Rama, Hare Hare

We will consider this mantra at length in chapter 3. When a mantra does become so repetitive, as, for example, being said with each breath, does it need to be accompanied by sincere intention with each repetition? Or is the mere repeating (as in *japa*) sufficient? For some Indians the mere repetition is all that is required. For example, within some Hindu and Buddhist practices the numinous sound of the mantra, correctly pronounced, is all that is needed. This approach will be developed in chapter 2.

The chanting of a sacred sound also has musical aspects. As sound emitted by humans, mantras must have some effect on the psychosomatic human structure—the experience of the unity of the mind and body. The fact that mantras produce vibrations that resonate through one's whole psychophysical nature did not escape the Indians. Some sounds may cause the body to vibrate in such a way as to awaken certain states of consciousness. Traditional music and religious chants in Western culture, Gregorian chant, and the modal chanting of the weekly portion from the Five Books of Moses and the Prophets as well as the daily chanting of the Ashrei (one of the most familiar composite prayers made up of Psalm 82:5, 144:15, 145, 115:18) hymn in Jewish worship also attempt to achieve exactly such results. Tibetan Buddhist chanting of the mantra OM MANI PADME HUM in the D major chord (the full chord being sung by each monk) is widely famous for the hair-raising-on-the-back-of-the-neck effect it produces in many hearers. These numinous overtones seem designed to awaken our sensitivity to overtones of sound and meaning surrounding us in the universe. Hindu OM chanting and *kirtan* singing along with Sikh *bajans* all seem to evoke similar effects and to be rooted somehow in mantra vibration. One Hindu school of Kashmir Saivism talks of a cosmic *spanda* or sound vibration which all mantras attempt to yoke to or sympathetically join. Even the preaching or exposition of a mantra by a skilled rhetorician can, providing the audience knows the mantra by heart, raise the psychological response of the crowd to new heights of numinous awareness. Then there is the Sufi master's mystic experience of a keynote Qur'anic mantra that sets him off into a burst of ecstatic revelatory interpretation. All of these will be given detailed study in chapter 3.

RITUAL USE OF *MANTRAS* IN HOMES AND TEMPLES

Mantras are not coined or spontaneously created. They are words, verses, or symbolic sounds that are transmitted and organized by a tradition. Even natural sounds become mantras only when they are taken up and given structure and context. They are not left at the disposal of the people to use them as they wish. In the Indian culture, for example, one does not choose one's own mantra but receives it ritually from a guru, who in turn received it from his teacher, and so on, backward in an infinite regress, since, for the Indian, the universe is beginningless. The mantra one receives from the guru is the particular word that draws one's consciousness directly into harmony with the universe, with the eternal. Similarly, the family in which one grows up and the temples one may attend, be they Saivite or Vaisnavite, will provide a cultural context for the passing on of specific mantras and rituals from generation to generation. Although some philosophical schools may consider mantras as divine word (*daivi vak*) innate within all human beings, still it is strongly argued that the traditions of the elders are the essential teachings for young children if these inherent mantras are to be successfully actualized. Bhartrhari's theory of language as daivi vak, examined in chapter 2, is a sophisticated presentation of this viewpoint from India's highly cultured Sanskrit tradition. Even Bhartrhari, with his view of the universal presence of divine word-consciousness, is quite clear that mantra chanting can lead one to release (moksa) only if the mantras learned are those of the Sanskrit culture of India presented in criterion form in the Vedas. Whatever else can be said about the significance of this teaching, it clearly shows the interconnectedness of life and the sacred character of tradition and authority.

When one enters a Hindu home in India, in America or, for that matter, anywhere in the world, one room or a quiet niche will be set aside as the worship space. To enter one must leave one's shoes at the door. The room will be empty except for a low altar upon which the Hindu images, preferred by the various family members, will be arrayed. Each morning the various images will be circled with a stick of burning incense while the mantra appropriate to the image is said. Mantra and darshan begin the day as the deity is wooed from sleep to be present through the morning prayer in temples, shrines, and households throughout India. The meaning of mantra as spiritual discipline, a discipline leading to a deep recognition of union with the divine, is vivid in these common acts.

Approaching a temple in India or America is an experience that seems quite foreign to any Western notion of "going to church." One's shoes must be left at the door. The temple is constructed in a series of outer porches in the shape of a *mandala* (a geometric map of the cosmos). At

FIGURE 1.6 A young Swami in his *puja* room, Kodaikanal, South India. COURTESY RONALD NEUFELDT

the center of the temple is the sanctum where the image is situated. On entering the temple one first circumambulates it through the exterior porches. On the walls carvings of images are observed so that the process of darshan, seeing the divine, already begins. Also in the outer porches temple musicians will be chanting mantras to aid the worshiper. Other devotees will be piously chanting mantras as they individually go about their worship. Unlike the Western practice of unified congregational activity, Hindu temple worship is an individual affair. The resonance of the chant of the musicians with the murmured prayers of many individual worshipers echoes through the high stone hallways. As one listens it blends into an antiphone of sacred sounds.

Approaching the sanctum or center of the temple one is struck by the dimness of the lighting. Unlike a Western church with its many windows, the sanctum of the Hindu temple is windowless, down some steps and deep within. Indeed it is called the *garbhagrha* or "womb chamber." It corresponds to the creative center of the universe. Consequently, the most

FIGURE 1.7 Temple procession paying respects to a wayside shrine, near Madras. COURTESY RONALD NEUFELDT

powerful mantra suited to the image is reserved for chanting as one approaches the image of the temple deity for darshan. In accordance with the deep mystery surrounding the image, mantras are mutely whispered. An air of charged stillness pervades. The combination of visual darshan and murmured mantras produces a simultaneous seeing and hearing that powerfully unites the devotee with the divine.

But how does the image in the sanctum (or in the household shrine) become a god or goddess in the first place? The deity is spoken into being through mantra. *Prana-pratistha* is the mantra used to install the deity. Through it the breath (*prana*), the vital energy of the cosmos is infused into what up to that moment has been simply a sculpture of the god or goddess. Here is the prana-pratistha mantra that infuses the cosmic energy of the divine and makes the sculpture a *murti*, a presence of the divine.

> *Am, Hrim, Krom, Srim, Svaha*: May the Life of this Devata be here: *Am, Hrim, Krom, Srim, Svaha*: May Her *Jiva* be here: *Am, Hrim, Krom, Srim, Svaha*: May all Her senses be here: *Am, Hrim, Krom, Srim, Svaha*: The Speech, Mind, Sight, Smell, Hearing, Touch, and the Vital Airs of the *Adya-Kalia* Devata, may they come here and stay happily here for ever: *Svaha*.[28]

This is followed with a mantra welcoming the deity as one would a friend, bidding that the deity be pleased and comfortable after the long journey. Now that the deity is present, now that the prana, the vital breath or cosmic energy of the deity, is recognized as present in the murti, that energy can be tapped through the specific mantras associated with the god or goddess. These specific mantras are used from then on in worship.

The mantras of the deity are the deity's sound body. The texts refer to deities as having a gross body, the murti, a sound body, the mantra, and a body manifest in geometrical design through *yantras* (mystic diagrams to channel psychic forces) and mandalas.

The newly installed deity, placed in the womb chamber of the temple, is understood to be newborn. The appropriate rites or samskaras for the newborn are administered with all the mantras and ritual acts that accompany their administration to a person. The samskaras for birth, naming, removal of the first hair, the first taking of solid food, are offered to the deity. The presence of the deity is real, as real as the presence of a newborn child. What is good and necessary for the newborn child is good and necessary for the deity. The samskaras identify the eternal elements and link the reality of the deity with the reality of the soul. In giving the prana-pratistha mantra and the samskaras to the murti, what is spoken to the deity is heard in the devotees from the god or goddess. What they say about the deity they hear about themselves. Just as this process of "god-making" involves calling the soul, jiva, and the senses of the deity to abide

FIGURE 1.8 Bathing the deity in the sanctum of the temple, near Madras. COURTESY RONALD NEUFELDT

in the murti—all highlighted in the prana-pratistha mantra—so the soul and senses of the devotee, through mantra, are purified and nurtured along the path to liberation.

All of this is at the heart of Hindu mantra practice. But in India we hear other mantras as well—especially those of the Sikhs who take much Hindu mantra influence into their own tradition. Thus we conclude this chapter with a brief note on the Sikh hearing of mantra.

In the Sikh temple (*gurdwara*) and the household shrine we find a regard expressed toward Sikh scripture, the Guru Granth Sahib, similar to that expressed by Hindus toward the murti in the Hindu temple. Guru Granth is the center of the devotee's attention. It is the Guru Granth as God that speaks the mantra, the Word of God.

Sikh faith developed through a succession of ten historical gurus beginning with Guru Nanak (1469–1538) and culminating in Guru Gobind Singh (1666–1708). In the Sikh tradition, unlike Hinduism, statues of deities and pictures of gurus were prohibited. Indeed, Guru Nanak saw

FIGURE 1.9 A Sikh devotee stands in reverence before the canopy protecting the Guru Granth Sahib in the gurdwara. COURTESY DAVID J. GOA

the possibilities of idolatry even of his own person and made a distinction between himself as God's mouthpiece and the message he uttered: "I spoke only when you, O God, inspired me to speak" (AG 566).[29] The emphasis is on *gurbani*, God's word spoken by the guru instead of an image. Although first spoken as oral revelations, the words were memorized and written down. Interestingly, they include the words of Hindu, Muslim, and Sikh holy men. The fifth guru, Arjun, compiled these utterances into the canonical collection, the Guru Granth Sahib.[30] Gobind Singh, the tenth guru, prepared the final recension of the Granth and, while dying, installed the written text as the living guru. Guru Granth is housed in its own building or room, the gurdwara. It is placed on a cushion, covered by a canopy, and wrapped in special cloths. It is physically located so that it will be in the most elevated position and, when being moved, it is carried on the head, all to indicate its exalted status as guru. Many of these practices have their roots in Hindu religious culture. Just as Hindus bow before the image of the deity, so Sikhs bow before the

Granth and are careful not to turn their backs to it. The book is ritually put to bed and awakened. Before entering a gurdwara one must have bathed, removed one's shoes, and covered one's head. Offerings are placed before the enthroned book and after worship a *prasad* is eaten. For many Sikhs the very sight of the scripture is a means of receiving grace. It is treated in this manner and is a means of grace precisely because it is the Guru Granth that speaks (as a living guru) the mantras, which wipe away ignorance and illumine consciousness.[31]

2

The Nature of Mantra

Scholars all around the world, from Plato in the *Republic* to Lao Tzu in the *Tao Te Ching*, have speculated on the nature of language. As special words of revelation and power, mantras have received careful analysis by the scholars of India. Speculations begin in the oldest Hindu scripture, the Rgveda, where language has a prominent place. The words or mantras of language are described as the support of gods such as Indra, Agni, and the Asvins. *Vak* (language) bends Rudra's bows against the skeptic and gathers up all prayers. In the Satapatha Brahmana Vak is identified with Sarasvati, who later becomes known as the goddess of learning, wisdom, and inspiration. The action of the rsis or sages in relation to the mantras of language is highlighted in Frits Staal's translation of Rgveda 10.71:

"Brhaspati! When they came forth to establish the first beginning of language, setting up names, what had been hidden in them as their best and purest good became manifest through love.

Where the sages fashioned language with their thought, filtering it like parched grain through a sieve, friends recognized their friendship. Their beauty is marked on the language.

They traced the course of language through ritual; they found it embodied in the seers. They gained access to it and distributed it widely; the seven chanters cheered them.

Many who look do not see language, many who listen do not hear it. It reveals itself like a loving and well adorned wife to her husband . . .

Though all the friends have eyes and ears, their mental intuitions are uneven. Some are like shallow ponds, which reach up to the mouth or armpit, others are like ponds which are fit for bathing."[1]

Here the power of language is clearly contrasted in its two forms. To those who "see," as Staal explains, language (and meaning) is a manifestation, is widely distributed by the rsis, is seen and heard with understanding, is self-revealing and provides for deep intuitions; in contrast, to those who do not "see," who are obstructed by their own ignorance, language is hidden, is mysteriously possessed by the rsis, is looked at and listened to without understanding, is wrongly used and is hidden in shallow intuitions. According to this hymn, the nature and function of language is to manifest or reveal the meaning of things.

The way in which mantras reveal the meaning and power of cosmic order (rta) is analyzed by various schools of Indian philosophy. Two principle schools, the Mimamsa and the Philosophy of Grammar, made the most significant contributions. Both of these schools follow the Brahmanic tradition stemming from the Veda, which takes language and mantras as of divine origin (daivi vak), as spirit descending and embodying itself in the vibrations of words. The well known Rgveda verse (4.58.3) expresses this truth in poetic form. It symbolizes Speech as the Bellowing Bull of abundant fecundity, as the Great God descending into the world of mortals. Patanjali, the great Grammarian scholar, asks, "Who is this Great God?" and answers, "Speech itself" (*mahan devah sabda*).[2] To this view of mantra the Hindu Mimamsa, Sankhya-Yoga, Grammarian, and Kashmir Saivism schools of philosophy are faithful.

In opposition to this high evaluation of mantra, there are the Indian schools that reject the Veda as an authoritative source of revelation—Jainism and Buddhism. Although the Jainas and the Buddhists adopted a naturalistic view of language, namely, that it is but an arbitrary and conventional tool, the chanting of mantras, as we shall see, continued to play an important role in Buddhist spiritual practice. But first let us examine the Hindu philosophical understandings of mantra arising from the Vedas.

Hindu thought sees a direct relationship between ritual action and mantras. Indeed, it has been suggested that in India language is not something with which you *name* something; it is something with which you *do* something.[3] Each spoken mantra corresponds to one ritual act. In post-Vedic India activities such as bringing the goddess Kali into a stone image, bathing to wash away sins, sowing seeds in the fields, guarding the sown seeds, driving away evil spirits, and meditating to achieve release, all had to be accompanied by the chanting of mantras in order to achieve success.[4] In some situations the ritual act itself was later modified or even abandoned, yet the action of mantra recitation was retained.[5] Within the ritual action it is the uttered mantra that has central importance for release (moksa).

THE MIMAMSA THEORY OF MANTRA AS ETERNAL WORD (*SABDA*)

The task of providing a theoretical explanation for the power of spoken mantras was taken up by the Mimamsa school of philosophy.[6] The Mimamsa proposed a theory of *sabda* that suggests that the sound produced in pronouncing a word is not the result of human choice or construction, rather, every sabda or word has an eternal meaning. Each sabda is the sound-representative of some aspect of the eternal cosmic order. The mantras of the Vedas, therefore, are not words coined by humans. They are the sounds or vibrations of the eternal principles of the cosmic order itself. It is for this reason that the rsis or speakers of the Vedas are called "seers" or "hearers" of the mantras and not the authors of the mantras. Thus the Hindu claim that the Vedas were not composed by human beings. They are not like other human literature. The Vedas, as the collection of the mantras, are not about everyday things. Rather, they give us negative and positive commands to ethical action in daily life that represent the eternal principles of rta (cosmic order) for ourselves and the universe around us. Even when the cosmic process ceases to be, between cycles of the universe, the mantras, as eternal truths, remain present in their seed state, ready to sound forth afresh as the eternal Veda in the next cycle of creation. Thus the mantras are said by the Mimamsakas to be authorless and eternal. Another important aspect of this view is that these mantras are not written but passed on orally. The Vedic mantras are, thus, the eternal sounds of the ethical truth of the universe and ourselves. Words other than the Vedic mantras were regarded as human-made, with their meanings being established by human convention and, thus, incapable of giving us ethical guidance. Only the meaning content of the Vedic mantras can teach us the required continuous ethical action and enjoyment of its fruits that is the end goal of life.

For the Mimamsakas the ultimate reality is nothing other than the eternal words of the Vedas. They did not accept the existence of a single supreme creator god, who might have composed the Veda. According to the Mimamsa these gods named in the Vedas have no existence apart from the mantras that speak their names. The power of the gods, then, is nothing other than the power of the mantras that name them.[7] This concept of sabda or word as divine, eternal, and authorless is given further development in the Grammarian notion of *Sabdabrahman* and in the Tantric notion of mantra as mystical sounds that are "vehicles of salvation (*mantrayana*)."[8] Patanjali's *Yoga Sutras* seem to take over the Mimamsa view with little change and then identify it with the mind of Isvara, the master yogi. Let us examine each of these in turn.

THE GRAMMARIAN THEORY OF MANTRA AS SABDABRAHMAN

We have seen that for the Mimamsa mantra is sabda, the eternal authorless words of the Veda. The Grammarians adopt all of this but add to it the notion of Brahman, God as unitary pure consciousness. Consequently the Grammarians offer a theory of mantra as a manifestation of Sabdabrahman or divine word-consciousness.[9] Although unitary in nature, this divine word-consciousness manifests itself in the diversity of words that make up speech. The mantra OM is identified as the root mantra out of which all other mantras arise.[10] This sacred syllable is held to have flashed forth into the heart of Brahman, while absorbed in deep meditation, and to have given birth to the Vedas, which contain all knowledge. OM and the Vedic mantras are described as being at once a means of knowledge and a way of release (moksa).[11] Fundamental to all of this is the notion that language and consciousness are inextricably intertwined. Indeed, the great Grammarian philosopher Bhartrhari puts it this way: "There is no cognition in the world in which the word does not figure. All knowledge is, as it were, intertwined with the word."[12] Bhartrhari goes on to make clear that the word-meaning, as the essence of consciousness, urges all beings toward purposeful activity. If the word were absent, everything would be insentient, like a piece of wood. Thus Bhartrhari describes the absolute or divine as Sabdabrahman (word-consciousness).[13]

When everything is merged into Sabdabrahman, as in a high moment of mystical experience, no speaking takes place and no meaning is available through mantras. But, when the divine is awakened and meanings are manifested through words, then the knowledge and power that is intertwined with consciousness can be clearly perceived and known. Because consciousness is of the nature of word-meaning, the consciousness of any sentient being cannot go beyond or lack word-meaning.[14] When no meaning is understood, it is not due to a lack of word-meaning in consciousness but rather to ignorance or absent-mindedness obscuring the meaning inherently present.[15] For Bhartrhari and the Grammarians, words (mantras), meanings, and consciousness are eternally connected and, therefore, necessarily synonymous. If this eternal identity were to disappear, knowledge, communion, and the means to spiritual release would all cease to exist.[16] T. R. V. Murti concisely sums up the Grammarian position when he says it is not that we have a thought and then look for a word with which to express it "or that we have a lonely word that we seek to connect with a thought. Word and thought develop together, or rather they are expressions of one deep spiritual impulse to know and to communicate."[17]

Some Indian theories of mantra take the view that mantras are meaningless. From the Grammarian perspective a meaningless mantra would imply a piece of consciousness without a word-meaning attached. According to Bhartrhari, that is impossible. It is possible, however, for a person to be obstructed by his or her own karmic ignorance and so not understand the meaning of a mantra—even though the word or words of the mantra are inherently meaningful. Let us take the word *love* as a mantra example. This word can be used in two ways: in one way it seems to be meaningless; in the other it overflows with meaning. When a young man and woman develop a deep, respectful, and trusting relationship, they may say "I love you" and call each other "my love." In so saying they express a fullness of meaning that no other word could better convey. Now imagine a couple in a divorce court, and the one says to the other, "Well, my love, let us separate." In the first case the word is a mantra evoking deep meaning. In the second case "my love" is a figure of speech that is no longer life giving. It had the potential to become a mantra but failed because of the couple's obscuring karma.

The reason for the speaking of mantras is also traced to the nature of word-consciousness by Bhartrhari. He states that word-consciousness itself contains an inner energy (*kratu*) that seeks to burst forth into expression.[18] For example, the rsis see the Veda as a unitary truth, but, for the purpose of manifesting that truth to others, they allow the word's inner energy to assume the form of the various mantras. On an everyday level this inner energy or kratu is experienced when, at the moment of having an insight or idea, we feel ourselves impelled to express it, to share it with others by putting it into words. Indeed, the whole activity of scholarship and teaching is dependent upon this characteristic of consciousness.

Bhartrhari offers a detailed analysis of how the uttered sounds of the mantra reveal meaning. He describes three stages in the speaking and hearing of mantras on the analogy of a painter.[19] Just as a painting is perceived as a whole over and above its different parts and colors, so our cognition of the mantra is of a meaning-whole over and above the sequence of uttered sounds. *Sphota* ("that from which meaning bursts or shines forth") is Bhartrhari's technical term designating mantra as a gestalt or meaning-whole that can be perceived by the mind as an immediate supersensuous intuition. Let us return to the example of the rsi. At the first moment of its revelation, the rsi is completely caught up in this unitary idea, gestalt, or sphota. But when under the expressive impulse (kratu) he starts to examine the idea (sphota) with an eye to its communication, he has withdrawn himself from the first intimate unity with the idea or inspi-

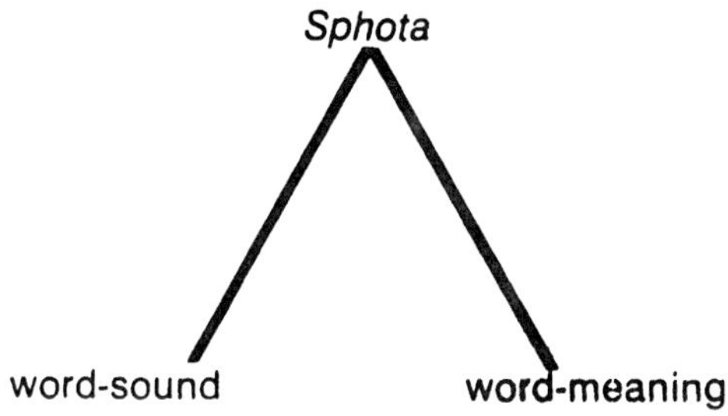

FIGURE 2.1

ration itself and now experiences it in a twofold fashion. On the one hand, there is the objective meaning, which he is seeking to communicate, and on the other are the words and phrases he will utter. For Bhartrhari these two aspects of word-sound and word-meaning, differentiated in the mind and yet integrated like two sides of the same coin, constitute the sphota. Bhartrhari emphasizes the meaning-bearing or revelatory function of this two-sided gestalt, the sphota, that he maintains is eternal and inherent in consciousness.[20]

For the person hearing a mantra the process functions in reverse. Each repetition of the mantra removes karmic ignorance and brings further illumination. After sufficient repetitions (depending on the darkness of the person's karma) the sphota of the mantra stands clearly perceived—perhaps something like the "light bulb coming on" image we find in cartoons. As Bhartrhari puts it: "The sounds, while they manifest the word, leave impression-seeds progressively clearer and conducive to the clear perception of the word."[21]

The logic of Bhartrhari's philosophy is that the whole is prior to the parts. This results in an ascending hierarchy of mantra levels. Individual words are subsumed by the sentence or poetic phrase, the phrase by the Vedic poem, and so on until all speech is identified with Brahman. But Bhartrhari focuses upon the *vakya-sphota* or sentence-meaning as the true form of meaning. Although he sometimes speaks about letter sounds or individual words as meaning-bearing units (sphota), it is clear that for Bhartrhari the true form of the sphota is the meaning-whole.[22] This has interesting implications for single-word mantras. Since the fundamental unit of meaning is a complete thought (vakya-sphota), single words must be single word sentences with the missing words being understood. For example, when the young child says "Mama," it is clear that whole ideas are being expressed, e.g., "I want mama." Even when a word is used merely in the form of a substantive noun (e.g., *tree*), the verb to be is always understood so that what is indicated is really a complete thought (e.g., "This is a tree").[23] In this fashion Bhartrhari suggests a way to understand single-word mantras as meaningful. A devotee chanting "Shiva" may well be evoking the meaning "Come Shiva" or "Shiva possess me" with each repetition. Thus, such single-word mantras are far from being meaningless. They invoke a world of meaning.

In Vedic ritual mantra is experienced on various levels, from the loud chanting of the priest to silently rehearsed knowledge of the most esoteric formulas.[24] Probably a good amount of the argument over the meaningfulness of mantras arises from a lack of awareness of the different levels of language. On one level there is the intuitive flashlike understanding of the meaning of the mantra as a whole. At this level the fullness of intuited meaning is experienced in the "seen" unity of sound and thought in sphota. This is the direct supersensuous perception of the truth of the mantra that occurs at the mystical level of language—when "mystical" is understood in its classical sense as a special kind of perception marked by greater clarity than ordinary sense perception.[25] Bhartrhari calls this level of mantra experience *pasyanti* (the seeing one)[26]—the full meaning of the mantra, the reality it has evoked, stands revealed. This is the rsi's direct "seeing" of truth and the Tantric devotee's visionary experience of the deity. Yet, for the uninitiated, for the one who has not yet had the experience, it is precisely this level of mantra that will appear to be nonexistent and meaningless. If, due to one's ignorance, the pasyanti level is obscured from "sight," then the uttering of the mantra will indeed seem to be an empty exercise.

Bhartrhari calls the level of the uttered words of the sentence *vaikhari*. At the vaikhari level every sound is inherently meaningful in that each sound attempts to reveal the sphota. Repetition of the uttered sounds of the mantra, especially if spoken clearly and correctly, will each time evoke the sphota afresh until finally the obscuring ignorance is purged and the meaning-whole of the mantra is seen. Between these two levels of uttering (vaikhari) and supersensuous seeing (pasyanti) there is a middle level of *madhyama* corresponding to the meaning-whole in its mental separation into meaning and a sequence of manifesting sounds, none of which have yet been uttered. For Bhartrhari the silent practice of mantra is accounted for by madhyama and is, of course, both real and meaningful.

When all three levels of language are taken into account, as they are by Bhartrhari, it would seem that all Vedic and Tantric types of mantra practice can be analyzed and shown to be meaningful. In cases where the karmic ignorance of the speaker or the hearer obstructs the evocative power of the mantra, it may indeed be experienced as meaningless. But even then the mantra is still inherently meaningful because it prepares the way for the sphota to be finally understood. Also there is the fact that the cultured person, not afflicted by ignorance, hears and understands the meaning even though the person uttering the mantra does not.[27] The argument, of course, is circular, and if it were merely a theoretical argument then Bhartrhari's explanation would have no power and would have been discarded long ago. However, Bhartrhari appeals not just to argument but also to empirical evidence—the direct perception of the meaning-whole (sphota) of the mantra. As long as such direct perception is reflected in the experience of people, Bhartrhari's explanation of the meaningfulness of mantras remains viable.

In the Indian experience the repeated chanting of mantras is an instrument of power.[28] The more difficulties there are to be overcome, the more repetitions are needed. Repeated use of correct mantras removes all impurities, purifies all knowledge, and leads to release. The psychological mechanism involved is described by Bhartrhari as a holding of the sphota in place by continued chanting. Just as from a distance or in semidarkness it takes repeated cognitions of an object before one sees it correctly, so also concentrated attention on the sphota by repeated chanting of the mantra results in the sphota finally being perceived in all its fullness.[29]

For Bhartrhari and the Grammarians, then, mantras are inherently meaningful, powerful in purging ignorance and revealing truth, and effective instruments for the realization of release (moksa). Indeed Bhartrhari's theory helps our modern minds to understand how the chanting of mantras can be experienced as meaningful, powerful, and in fact a "yoga of the word."[30]

MANTRA THEORY IN PATANJALI'S *YOGA SUTRAS*

Patanjali, the great systematizer of the Yoga school,[31] shares much in common with Bhartrhari, the Grammarian, when it comes to the understanding of mantra. In Patanjali's *Yoga Sutras*[32] Isvara, like Sabdabrahman, is described as an eternal unity of meaning and consciousness from which all speech, including the Vedic mantras, evolves.[33] Mantra, as the scriptural truth of the rsis, is taken to be the authoritative verbalization of Isvara's word-consciousness. All this is expressed in the sacred mantra, OM, which, when spoken, connotes Isvara and his omniscient consciousness. As was the case for Bhartrhari, it is the obscuring power of consciousness veiled by karmic ignorance that robs mantras of their inherent meaning and power.[34] And as was the case for Bhartrhari, Patanjali states that this ignorance can be removed through a constant repetition of appropriate Vedic mantras. Says Patanjali, as a result of constant chanting or study (*svadhyaya*) upon mantras (including seed or *bija* syllables like OM) the desired deity becomes visible.[35] Through the practice of fixed concentration (*samadhi*) upon an object, in this case an uttered mantra, consciousness is purified of karmic obstructions and the deity "seen." Since for Patanjali OM is the mantra for Isvara, the devotee is advised that the *japa* or chanting of OM will result in the clear understanding of its meaning. Vyasa, a commentary on Patanjali, puts it in more psychological terms:

> The yogi who has come to know well the relation between word and meaning must constantly repeat it [the mantra] and habituate the mind to the manifestation therein of its meaning. The constant repetition is to be of the *pranava* (OM) and the habitual mental manifestation is to be that of what it signifies, *Isvara.* The mind of the Yogi who constantly repeats the *pranava* and habituates the mind to the constant manifestation of the idea it carries, becomes one-pointed.[36]

What does it mean for the mind to become "one-pointed"? The "point" is the mantra that is being chanted. "One-pointed" means that the continual chanting of the mantra is keeping it front and center in one's mind to the exclusion of everything else one might perceive or think. Through the chanting the devotee has become one with the mantra (OM in this case). It is as though one's whole world becomes only the mantra and for the period of the chanting nothing else exists. It is like the experience we sometimes have when we find ourselves "caught up" in a piece of music to which we are listening—for the moment your hearing of the music fills the whole universe. Or it is like the experience of being in a moment of love or sexual intercourse with another person—for the moment everything else ceases to exist. You are one pointed. The yoga discipline described here involves becoming one pointed or one with the mantra OM and what it signifies, Isvara.

The power of such mantra concentration (samadhi) to induce a perfectly clear identity with the signified deity is given detailed psychological analysis in the commentary on *Yoga Sutra* 1:42. With continued mantra concentration all traces of uttered sounds and conceptual meaning are purged until only the direct pure perception of Isvara remains. Patanjali's analysis supports Bhartrhari's claim that the repetition of mantra samadhi has the power to remove ignorance and reveal truth.[37] This conclusion confirms the Vedic mantra experience (previously discussed) and the Tantric mantra experience to which we will turn shortly.

As an additional aspect of the practice of mantra concentration and chanting, Patanjali prescribes the yogic discipline of making Isvara the motive of all one's actions (*Isvarapranidhanam*).[38] It is as though one is to become an "empty channel" through which Isvara (who is being held steady at the center of one's mind through the chanting or meditation upon OM) acts. In one's yoga practice one is attempting to emulate Isvara, the master yogi, so what better way than to attempt to act in every situation as though he were acting through you? It is rather like the young hockey player who tries to keep Gretzky uppermost in his mind so that as he goes down the ice all his moves will be those of the "great one." While chanting OM one "dedicates" all one's moves to Isvara. The result of such complete self-surrender, says the yoga text, is a vision of Isvara. In this way the yoga of Patanjali is perhaps the oldest statement of theistic mantra meditation.[39] It is this actual face-to-face encounter with God that is given further development in theistic mantra meditation.

Theistic Mantra Meditation

The theistic traditions (e.g., worship of Shiva or Vishnu), which come to dominate Hinduism, use the meditation on mantras to effect an actual encounter with God. In the devotee who reverently disposes him or herself to an experience of transcendence, the mantra functions to take one out of or beyond one's spirit to an existential experience of the divine. The mantra has a sacramental function to make God present as an actual event. In Hindu theistic experience mantras have both meaning and power—power to purify the mind and reveal the transcendent lord to the devotee in an existential encounter.[40]

Such mantras in the Hindu theistic traditions are held to have been created by the decree of the god involved—Shiva in the above examples. Shiva creates and empowers these mantras to be effective in communicating himself to his devotees for their salvation or release. When the practice of mantra chanting is put together with a concentrated seeing of the image of Shiva, the result is a powerful opening of the mind of the devotee in surrender to the god who is mediated through both sound and sight. Taken together, the mantra and the image have great power to remove distractions or mental impurities and open the way to a direct hearing and seeing of the divine.

MANTRA THEORY IN THE TANTRIC TRADITION

Unlike the philosophical and religious schools we have examined, Tantrism is a pan-India movement in that it is assimilated by all the great Indian religions (Hinduism, Buddhism, and Jainism) and by the various philosophical schools. There is a Buddhist Tantrism, a Hindu Tantrism, and to some extent even the Jainas adopt Tantric methods. Strong Tantric influences are present in the Hindu sectarian movements of Saivism and

Vaisnavism. According to Eliade, Tantrism begins to flower in fourth-century India and assumes a pan-Indian vogue from the sixth century onward.[41] What is the place of mantra in this new movement? Whereas the Vedic mantras serve to link the worshiper with the divine and to define the complex order (rta) of the universe, the Tantric mantra aims at the annihilation of all distinctions and the affirmation of the worshiper's identity with the divine. "The *mantras* reflect this simplified worldview, recognizing fewer distinct beings, focusing on the one relation of man to God, and attempting to express sonically the collapse of the manifest universe into a single category."[42] While the various Vedic mantras deal with different relationships between ourselves and the cosmic order (rta), the Tantric liturgy works to have us realize the one all-encompassing relationship, namely, worshiper = ritual = God. The divine, the worshiper, and the ritual all become one in the chanting of the mantra. While this bears much similarity with Grammarian and Yoga theory, which we have seen, there is one unique aspect that Tantrism highlights, namely, the power and function of the Great Goddess. No longer is the female merely an aspect that comes out of the male God, now the Goddess and her power (*Sakti*) are identified with the divine. And it is this female Sakti that the Tantric mantras seek to realize.[43] Particularly in Hinduism, Sakti is elevated to the rank of the Divine Mother who sustains the universe and all its beings, including the gods. As the Great Goddess, woman incarnates the ultimate being of the universe: the great mystery of creation, living, dying, and being reborn. When danger threatens the cosmic order (rta), the gods appeal to Sakti the Great Goddess to put things right. And she usually does so, with a vengeance. Feminine divinities also made their way into Buddhism[44] along with a focus upon the natural realities of life (eating, having sex, wearing clothes, and so on) as means of approaching and uniting oneself with the divine. Speech and sound, along with the rhythms of breathing, are natural processes upon which Tantric practice placed great emphasis. Another rule of Tantrism, however, is that the Tantric path begins with an initiation by a teacher or guru—one who knows all the secrets and can communicate them to you only from mouth to ear.

Eliade states, "It was tantrism, especially, Buddhistic as well as Sivaistic, that raised the mantras and *dharanis* to the dignity of a vehicle of

FIGURE 2.2 Phadoung Kakulphimph, a devotee of the Theravada Buddhist tradition, practices meditation in his home in Canada. PHOTOGRAPH AARON GOOS; COURTESY OF THE FOLKLIFE PROGRAM, PROVINCIAL MUSEUM OF ALBERTA

salvation (*mantrayana*)."[45] The term *dharani* literally means "she who upholds or encloses." They are sometimes partial or mutilated words (e.g. *vimale, hime, kale*) that express ideas of purity, but the majority of them are phonemes that seem to generate an inner echo when chanted during meditation (e.g. *hrim, hram, hrum*).[46] Dharanis and mantras have to be specially received from the mouth of one's guru. They are thus different from the ordinary words that make up ordinary language or that we read in books. Once given by a guru, however, a mantra or dharani is claimed to have great power. Correctly pronounced and spoken according to the instructions (usually in synchronization with one's rhythm of respiration), union with Sakti, Shiva, or Buddhahood may be attained. That the final goal could apparently be attained simply by repeated chanting seemed an easy path and this may at least partly account for the popularity of Tantrism right up to the present. Although it looks easy from the outside, this easiness is more apparent than real. Tantra, like the other yogas of India, is a long and difficult path. For example, uttering the mantra must be preceded by purification of thought. While speaking, one must concentrate on each of the letter sounds composing the mantra, avoid fatigue, and so on, observes Eliade.

In the Tantric view the power of mantras is that they can become the "objects" they represent. "Each god, for example, and each degree of sanctity have a *bija-mantra*, a 'mystic sound' which is their 'seed,' their 'support'—that is, their very being."[47] Each deity, suggests Bharati, has his or her bija-mantra often formed from the first three letters of the deity's name, e.g., GAM for Ganesha, DUM for Durga, etc. By correctly chanting such a bija-mantra the devotee directly participates in its essence. He or she becomes the god or state of spiritual sanctity. In this sense the mantras are symbols that participate in that to which they point. The entire sonic universe, with all its gods, planes, and modes of being is manifested in a certain number of mantras. By chanting the mantra one awakens all the cosmic forces that correspond to it. The Tantric assumption is that there is a perfect correspondence between particular letter sounds (with accompanying image and color) and particular planes or degrees of sanctity. By chanting the sound that symbolizes it, the devotee evokes a particular plane of sanctity within his or her experience. The chanted sounds allow the devotee to assimilate the ontological state that he or she wishes to acquire. The Tantric worldview organizes these various ontological planes in a hierarchical continuity—each plane being correlated with a subtle center in the human body (the *Kundalini cakras*) and a bija-mantra. For example the bija-mantra *Hang* evokes the god Shiva in his androgynous form and is physically centered in the *visuddha* cakra located in the throat.[48] (A complete chart of the cakras is presented in figure 2.3.) In this way a systematic mechanism is presented by which the devotee, under the guidance of a guru, can, through mantra chanting, awaken the various centers and experience identity with the spiritual planes or realities each center evokes. Eventually, identity with the whole cosmos may be realized.

The Tantric bija-mantras are also seen to function as a "shorthand" for metaphysical systems. This is especially the case for Buddhism, says Eliade,

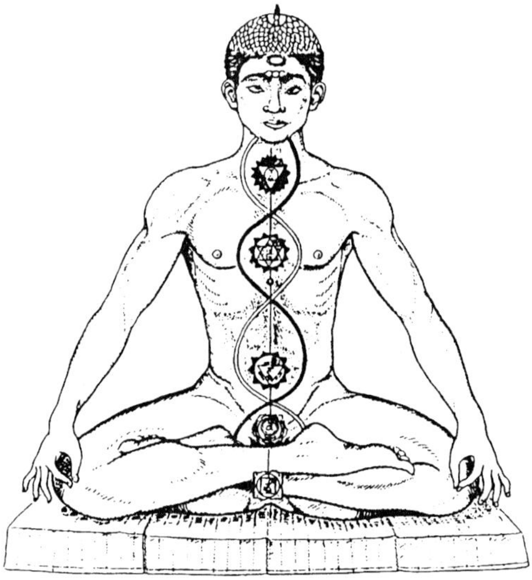

FIGURE 2.3

where the eight thousand stanzas of a voluminous Mahayana text, the *Astasahasrika-prajna-paramita* were summarized in a few stanzas that were then further reduced to the few lines of the *prajna-paramita mantra* and finally reduced further to a single seed or bija-mantra: *pram.*[49] Thus, by chanting *pram,* one could be evoking in shorthand the whole of the Mahayana prajna-paramita metaphysics. This seems parallel to the Hindu practice encountered earlier where the chanting of the seed syllable OM was thought of as evoking the whole of the Veda. Some scholars have referred to such seed syllables as being meaningless or empty of meaning.[50] Rather, it is their fullness of meaning—the whole meaning of the Vedas or the prajna-paramita—that is evoked by the chanting of the seed mantra. Indeed, it has been suggested that mantric utterances should be thought of as cognitive tools—as mental mechanisms for thinking a certain privileged class of thoughts.[51] In this sense a mantra functions something like a mathematical formula, meaningless to the uninitiated but evoking deep insight to those who understand. The powerful mantra ARAM brings to the Shiva devotee the insight and direct realization "I am Shiva!" The various theoretical analyses of mantra offered in this chapter have made clear that the term *mantra* is not just a word or verse of scripture. It is that and something more—the divine truth in which the words and all of life partake.

3

Finding One's Mantra

We said earlier that in India, from a mother's womb to the funeral pyre, one literally lives and dies in mantra. Having examined some of the theories of mantra in the preceding chapter we want now to sample some of the life experiences of mantra in India and America. These range from the traditional initiation of an individual by a guru to hearing a mantra preached in a large congregation and, finally, to the singing of sacred mantras by Hindus, Buddhists, Muslims, and Sikhs. In addition we will look at the significance of mantra for the recovery of contemplative prayer in Christianity. Each of these experiences exemplifies different ways in which the divine is heard through mantras. Taken together they provide a menu of different ways in which one may find one's own mantra. They also indicate the social context in which people grow up and learn mantra practice by osmosis, as it were. As Harvey Alper has pointed out, the routine use of mantras presupposes specific convictions concerning the human condition, the ideal social order, and the purpose of existence.[1] Acceptance of these convictions provides the social and religious basis that has made and continues to make mantra practice possible. Although, as we saw in chapter 2, reasons may be offered to defend these convictions, they are also simply the social patterns and rituals within which life in India is lived. The uttering of mantras would seem to be the most characteristic Hindu ritual gesture.

As we have seen, mantra chanting is essential to ritual action in Vedic, Yogic, and Tantric settings. Just as the gurus and the devotees following the final two stages of life complete everyday experience by transcending it, so too the chanting, preaching, or singing of mantras may be understood to complete our everyday use of language by transcending it. Thus mantras have both a social and individual function. In the earlier life stages, as, for example, in family and public rituals, they function as a kind of "sonic glue" to hold society together. In the later stages the mantras become highly refined instruments of personal inner transformation—transformation of exactly the kind that the earlier householder stage values and looks forward to as the ultimate completion of one's spiritual growth. In this sense mantras are not just mystical instruments of individual spiritual practice, they also form the basis of public worship or puja. Thus mantras function at the intersection of "public" and "private" life in India. Indeed, the genius of Indian mantra practice is that even when it is used as a basis for withdrawal from ordinary worldly life, as in the last two stages of life, it is still affirming the order and values of everyday existence, for it is the expected and hoped for goal. Hence the joyful willingness of a family and village to provide food and shelter for the old uncle who has retired from his daily life as a lawyer to spend the last half of his life in increasingly private mantra chanting. His action is not seen as selfishness or as a drain on society, as it might well be judged in the modern West. Instead, his family and village take pride in the fact that one of their number is living out their social and religious ideal. Although transcending everyday life, the old uncle is also confirming it by being a living exemplification of its ideals.

Having a "living ideal" in one's midst also serves to keep one's lower and very worldly values of material possessions and sensual enjoyments in their proper perspective—namely, appropriate and necessary for the householder stage but not the values to which one should become permanently attached. Ultimately material and sensual attachment must be transcended in the isolated spiritual life of a *sannyasin.* But to make such a transition one must find one's own mantra, and that can only be done under the guidance of a guru.

FIGURE 3.1 Elderly yogi who has devoted himself to study and meditation. COURTESY RONALD NEUFELDT

FINDING ONE'S MANTRA THROUGH A GURU

One of the most ancient and important patterns present in Indian society is the receiving of one's mantra from a guru. Although many manuals on mantras and their use may be found in India, mantra practice is never just a matter of the mechanical application of the rules found in such manuals. Rather, it depends on careful guidance by one's guru or spiritual master. Even in Tantric settings, which are sometimes more flexible, the use of a mantra is almost never "freelance."[2] Indian teaching has always maintained that mantras lose their power if not revealed by a guru and, indeed, that their unsupervised use may be dangerous. Mantras are the sound body of the deity, of cosmic energies, and it is necessary to balance these energies with the karmic predilections of the person. The central act of the guru is to bring about that balance, and so the "choice" of mantra is significant and particular indeed. The wrong mantra deepens instability or disharmony within. The right mantra guides one in another step toward union with the divine. And the question of which mantra is appropriate is really a question about what one's spiritual needs are. The guru is involved in the cure of persons; the guru is a spiritual physician.

It is not uncommon in India for people to have several gurus in their lifetime, although one guru will be of ultimate value for final release. Many Indians have also spoken about chosen gurus who in the end turned out to be the wrong ones for them. The mantras employed under such a guru deepened disharmony. The guru apparently did not properly understand the source of disharmony within the person. In such cases the guru is clearly not the proper guru, the one who can reach within and discern what is needed for liberation. Infatuation governed the devotee's choice. Finally, when the right guru is found—or finds the devotee, as many say—the movement toward harmony and release is immediate.

It is for this reason that the Indian tradition has maintained that mantras are esoteric knowledge that should be kept secret. Consequently, says Bharati, many traditional manuals were written in such a way that the mantra was spelled out in a disguised fashion that only an initiate would understand.[3] More recently, however, a mantra manual has been assembled that presents an encyclopedic compilation of Hindu mantras in straightforward fashion with no attempt at disguise.[4] This new manual, widely used in cities like Mumbai, offers an indication of how modern influences are altering traditional mantra practice.

A traditional view, however, of the role of the guru is presented in the Kashmiri Saivite text *Sivasutravimarsini* by Ksemaraja (ca. eleventh century C.E.). The text states, "If one doesn't understand the hidden sense of a mantra, one will have to surrender to an authentic master."[5] It goes on to add that when it comes to making mantras work it is the guru who is the path. The guru is seen as the supreme mediator between the ordinary and the divine. As the text puts it, "It is the guru who is the supreme passageway (*tirtha*), in comparison to him any other passageway is of no use."[6] As a passageway to the divine the combination of the guru's image and speech is especially powerful:

The guru's form (*murti*) is the source of trance (*dhyana*),
the guru's foot is the source of ritual action (*puja*);

The guru's utterance (*vakya*) is the source of mantra,
the guru's compassion (*krpa*) is the source of freedom (*moksa*).[7]

To find one's mantra, one must first find one's guru. From the guru one will receive the mantra specially selected to remove one's own impurities or karmic obstructions and advance one toward the realization of moksa or release.

As a perfected spiritual master, the guru's mind is completely pure and transparent (*sattvic*). Thus, when the devotee and the guru meet, the transparent mind of the guru is superimposed upon the devotee's mind with its ego-knots of karmic obstruction from actions in this and previous lives—and these are what the guru "sees." Having a clear understanding of the devotee's problem, the guru, like a doctor, prescribes the precise mantra that has the power to remove the particular karmic obstruction. When, after sufficient mantra chanting, that particular obstruction is removed, there is a direct realization of the divine and of spiritual freedom. The guru's prescription of a mantra has effectively transformed the devotee from the beginning state of a consciousness dominated by worldly concerns to a final state in which the mantra evokes a full and complete experience of the divine. However, this may well have required many years of chanting the mantra by the devotee. Then, in the context of the text we are discussing, one has become equivalent to Shiva and all one's speaking is the repetition of Shiva's name. Ksemaraja, author of the text, explains: "[The discourse of a master is japa] because he truly has constant inner realization of being the supreme 'I.' This is in accordance with the maxim: I myself am the supreme Hamsa, Siva, the primal cause."[8] So one sign of the highest spiritual attainment is the constant japa or muttering of sacred syllables. But of course the context is important. Under the prescription of the guru, if I were directed to utter the mantra HAMSA eighteen thousand times, the first utterance ought to be qualitatively different from the last. The point of the endless repetition would be for me as a devotee not just to lose myself in trance but to remove the last karmic impurity and have the inner revelation of being Shiva. Our text summarizes as follows:

> *Japa* is the progressive realization of the supreme state;
> It is precisely this-one's own primeval sound which is a mantra—that is to be repeated (*jap*);
> With the letter *sa* [the breath] is expelled, with the letter *ha* it reenters;
> The individual being constantly repeats the mantra, "*hamsa, hamsa.*"
> Day and night, 21,600 [times] this repetition [of the mantra] of the goddess is enjoined;
> It is simple to achieve this, but difficult for dullards.[9]

The committing of oneself to such a rigorous spiritual discipline is a serious matter. It is marked by the ceremony of diksa or initiation of the devotee by a guru. The word diksa is defined by Bharati as dedication of oneself to the undertaking of religious practices, self-devotion to a person or god, or exclusive occupation with a spiritual goal.[10] The most important aspect of diksa however, is the receiving of a mantra from the guru. The mantra provides the content of the diksa or initiation.[11] The practice of receiving a specially chosen mantra from a guru in an initiation ceremony is common to Hinduism, Buddhism, Jainism, and even to some tribal practice in India. Such a ceremony is always a one-to-one interpersonal process between one guru and one disciple.[12] The key part of this ceremony occurs when the guru whispers the mantra individually selected to suit the needs of a particular devotee into his or her ear.

Any practicing Hindu may receive mantra-diksa or initiation with a mantra. A person may go to a hereditary or family guru, or a person may "shop around." In the latter case the procedure is as follows. A person feels the desire for "spiritual practice" and goes to several teachers and listens to them. The guru whose teaching and personality have the most appeal is singled out. The devotee then tries to get that teacher interested in him or her by visiting frequently, bringing gifts of food and clothing, and discussing the possibility of diksa. When the guru feels the time is ripe, an auspicious day is selected when, according to the horoscopes of all involved, the particular deity desired will be easily accessible for worship. It is at this time that the mantra of the deity, as selected by the guru, is imparted to the disciple.

But before this time the disciple has had to prepare properly. This involves fasting for twelve hours, taking a bath, and bringing some fruits or other presents as a sacrificial fee to the guru's place. The guru sits facing East or South with the disciple facing him. The guru's deity is first invoked and then the disciple is instructed on the modes of worship: keeping the mantra secret, breath control (*pranayama*), and concentrating the mind on one point (*dharana*)—the one point in this case being the mantra. It is expected that the *asana* or sitting posture will have been mastered before the diksa or initiation takes place. The guru then "whispers the *mantra* into the disciple's right ear repeating it three times, and has it repeated three times by the disciple, first singly, then at one stretch."[13] The mantra must not be written down by the disciple or it will lose its power. Nor can it be passed on by the disciple to another person. Only after the disciple has achieved spiritual perfection and become a guru is he or she in a position to pass on mantras to others, and then it will be through the diksa or initiation ritual we have just described. After the mantra has been received, the disciple prostrates before the guru by lying face down on the ground with the forehead touching the guru's feet. The disciple then rises, circumambulates the guru three times, receives some sanctified food (*prasad*) from the guru, worships at the shrine, takes another bath, and withdraws.

The giving of the Gayatri Mantra with the sacred thread (described in chapter 1) is a different kind of initiation from the Tantric diksa ceremony described above. The Vedic Gayatri is a standard mantra given to all boys of the upper three castes and was seen as an initiation that allowed him to master the Vedic knowledge needed for successfully entering the role of a householder. In Vedic times girls also were initiated.[14] By contrast to the Vedic Gayatri , the diksa initiation is most appropriate for those who have completed the householder stage and are dedicating themselves to the final goal of complete spiritual realization appropriate to the final two stages of life, the forest dweller and the sannyasin or holy wanderer. In the diksa initiation there is no common mantra, but, as described above, the guru carefully selects the appropriate mantra for the life situation or karma of each devotee.

Many Indians have a guru whom they may know and consult with in the flesh, while others may have a guru who died years ago or decades before the devotee was born. Their relationship to the guru, however, is no less intimate. The relationship is eternal in character and not bound by the normal understanding of time and space. We see a striking parallel with the relationship some pious Christians have with saints. The needs of one's soul are spoken to across time. The life of the soul does not know the bonds of death.

In the 1960s gurus began arriving in America from India bringing mantra practice, customized for Americans, with them. One of the first was Maharishi Mahesh Yogi who taught a simple mantra meditation that he called Transcendental Meditation—often referred to as TM. He was widely recognized as the guru of the Beatles. The Maharishi, as he became known, started a university-based movement called the Students' International Meditation Society (SIMS) and soon had SIMS centers in over a thousand North American colleges and universities. Eck notes, "By the early 1980s, the society estimated that more than 1.5 million Americans had received a mantra and begun practicing TM under a teacher's instruction."[15] There are now TM centers spread across North America, and a university, the Maharishi University of Management in Fairfield, Iowa. Transcendental Meditation describes its approach as a simple, natural, easily learned mental technique of mantra meditation for fifteen to twenty minutes twice daily, sitting comfortably with the eyes closed. A mantra specially suited to the karma of the person is given by the TM teacher at the time of initiation. By following TM mantra practice, it is claimed, the meditator is able to realize a natural state of blissful relaxed yet fully alert consciousness. No difficult postures, special clothing, or cushions are required. One simply sits in a chair at home to do the TM mantra meditation. And it is open to everyone regardless of age, education, culture, or religion. In simplifying and adapting Hindu mantra practice for America, the Maharishi demonstrated a keen understanding of the American mind.

FIGURE 3.2 Devotees seek guidance and blessings from their guru and from priests particularly during rituals associated with their mantra. COURTESY RONALD NEUFELDT

Introductory sessions were free, but for those wanting to go on and receive training, initiation, and their own mantra there was sufficient cost to make them take it seriously—to put in their twenty minutes of mantra meditation a day so as to get their "money's worth." In India the tradition is that gurus take on students and prescribe mantras without charge.

In the stress-filled, overly busy American lifestyle, TM has brought immediate benefit to large numbers of people. Mantra meditation using the TM approach has been scientifically proven to slow down one's metabolism and induce a state of relaxation that reduces blood pressure and releases stress. Rather than using the language of Hindu philosophy and religion, TM has adapted the language of modern science to describe its results. Today TM in America is practiced by corporate executives, lawyers, school teachers, military persons, and many others who claim that TM improves their health and their job performance; TM mantra meditation seems to appeal to the American desire to have a practical approach to spirituality.[16]

A quite different Indian mantra practice was brought to America in 1965 by A. C. Bhaktivedanta. Rather than adapting traditional practice to America, as the Maharishi did with TM, Bhaktivedanta retained the full Hindu approach to devotional or bhakti mantra chanting and also achieved success. From his humble beginning chanting "Hare Krishna, Hare Rama" in New York's Tompkins Square Park, Bhaktivedanta soon began to attract followers to his joyful, colorful, ecstatic chanting. Soon he opened his first Krishna temple in a Second Avenue storefront on the Lower East Side. In five years he and his followers had temples in some thirty American cities. His movement was named the International Society for Krishna Consciousness (ISKCON). Unlike TM, this was not a comfortable use of mantra practice that meshed easily with North American life. Rather, ISKCON introduced a very traditional Hindu devotional approach with a completely different worldview and lifestyle involving Hindu dress, worship, chanting, singing, and dancing. Yet Bhaktivedanta, with his counterculture and fervent piety, succeeded in attracting a dedicated group of young followers that steadily increased in size during the 1970s and 1980s, spreading their message everywhere from "drug row" and working-class streets to university campuses.

Bhaktivedanta followed the approach of Caitanya, a sixteenth-century ecstatic saint who lived in Bengal, India and popularized a form of mantra worship called *kirtan*—the chanting and singing of the Lord Krishna's holy name, e.g., "Hare Krishna, Hare Krishna, Krishna, Krishna, Hare, Hare." This devotional practice could be done by anyone regardless of caste, gender, or financial status. "The singing of God's name required only love and broke down the barriers that divided people from one another. The followers of Chaitanya were not only caste Hindus but untouchables, even Muslims."[17] It was this approach which Bhaktivedanta introduced to America with its rigorous discipline and demand for complete commitment. Devotees rise at dawn and chant the name of Krishna in traditional temple rituals involving the offering of food, flowers, water and sweets to the divine presence of Krishna so that the Lord's grace may be received in return. After offering food and fruit to Krishna, they eat together what has been consecrated by his presence. Incense is lit and used to circle the image of Krishna as mantra chanting of the Lord's name continues. This sensuous approach to mantra involving not only sound but also sight, smell, movement, and dancing has saved many young Americans from lives they described as filled with drugs and meaninglessness.

Although it never attracted the large numbers of TM, ISKCON, with its demanding lifestyle, has become a permanent part of American religious culture. Senior devotees of the Hare Krishna movement have gone on to become serious scholars of Hinduism, undertaking graduate studies at universities such as Harvard. Dressed in their orange-colored robes, senior ISKCON leaders participate regularly in scholarly interfaith organizations such as the Society for Hindu-Christian Studies, which meets annually with the American Academy of Religion. At the grassroots level the Hare Krishna temples have found themselves serving not only American converts but also the needs of Hindu immigrants who settled in America in significant numbers during the 1970s and 1980s. To begin with, the Hare Krishna temples were the only Hindu worship places to be found in local communities. When the Hindu immigrants showed up there on Sunday afternoons to engage in devotion to Lord Krishna, they would find a worship service in which they felt quite at home, complete with mantra chanting and a lecture on the Gita delivered by a well-trained Caucasian devotee dressed in the ochre robes of a Hindu monk.[18] Thus, the newly arrived Hindu immigrants could enjoy a fairly traditional Hindu worship followed by a vegetarian meal served Indian cultural style. In addition, ISKCON temples observe the birthday of Krishna, the Diwali festival of lights, and other festivals that made the Hindu immigrants feel that they had found something of their religious and cultural identity in America. By the 1990s, when the American-born children of the Hindu immigrants were coming of age, ISKCON played another role—namely, interpreting Hindu mantra theory and practice to second generation South Asian young people in a way more in tune with their American upbringing. For example, traditional Indian-born temple priests speak in Hindi or Punjabi in a free-floating style that does not appeal to American-born South Asians because their Indian language skills are not well developed and the dry delivery bores them. In contrast, ISKCON, under the guidance of its American-born swamis, reaches out to young people by presenting its message through plays, social gatherings, and lively debates in everyday English, led by the swami. Further, ISKCON swamis encourage young people to question and ask for explanations during daily talks—an openness not always experienced in traditional Hindu religious teaching.

In the Sikh tradition we find a somewhat different understanding of guru. All mantras come from the ten historical gurus and are given by the Guru Granth Sahib, Sikh scripture—itself seen as a living guru.

The seed mantra is *Nam.* Guru Nanak, the founder of the Sikh faith, taught that the sole necessity for men and women for the fullness of life was Nam, the meditation on the name of God. Through Nam union with God is given, and the cycle of birth and rebirth is broken and moksa attained. What is Nam? Guru Nanak suggested that Nam is the manifestation of God. Meditation on Nam is the path, the unity of divine presence.

The second mantra that all Sikh gurus and devotees use expands on Nam. When devotees come for initiation or *amrit* they come chanting, "Sat Guru Wahiguru" (the true name, wonder of God). *Wahiguru* proclaims God as the guru, and in the very sound of this mantra the vibration of life is said to reside. It is the basic mantra of the one God, the eternal absolute, and was chanted by the ten historical gurus. The devotees understand it as a way to engage God at the deepest levels of consciousness. As a mantra it has the power to remove darkness, ignorance, and attachments, all that prevents direct communion with God, the *Sat Guru.* Such mantra chanting marks the start of each day for the devout Sikh. In America this "prayer chanting" occurs each morning on the twenty-four-hour Punjabi-language radio stations such as the one in Blaine, Washington.

A Sikh receives a word as personal mantra when the Guru Granth Sahib

FIGURE 3.3 Many of the mantras beloved to Sikh devotees come directly from hymns in the Guru Granth Sahib, read and sung in public worship. COURTESY DAVID J. GOA

is opened at random and the word from this living guru is read and heard. Although this process of "taking God's word," *vak lao*, occurs in every Sikh service, including daily devotions when Guru Granth is read, it is most looked for during the amrit or baptism ritual. In the context of baptism when they are asked if they are willing to give up everything and be solely devoted to God, when they are asked with the words of Guru Nanak and Guru Gobind Singh if they are willing to "give their head" to the guru, they anticipate that singular word that Guru Granth will have for them on this day.

At the culmination of the ritual the Guru Granth Sahib is opened at random and is read from the first verse on the top left page. Just as a guru through divine knowledge of the karma of the devotee in a Hindu setting would choose the right portion of God's truth to speak to that karmic condition, so for Sikhs divine inspiration operates through this apparently random selection to choose the needed word appropriate for those who have come for amrit. This word, when spoken, is heard by the newly baptized ones as God's word, a mantra for them.

Baptism is built on an event in 1699 when Guru Gobind Singh, in the context of the gathered Sikh community of India, asked who would come forward and offer their heads to the guru. He brandished his sword and called for the head of a Sikh with the words of Nanak, "If you want to play the game of love, come to me with your head on your palm." Everyone was aware, of course, that Gobind Singh's father, the ninth guru, had been beheaded by the Mogul ruler because he refused to deny his faith. The five Sikhs who eventually came forward and offered their heads were taken into the guru's tent, beheaded, as tradition would have it, and came out eventually with the persona of the guru. They were transformed. They had given up all their own egotistical concerns, given their heads on their palms, as it were, and were seen to be as the guru.

Following the form of this event, amrit requires that the devotee let go of all egotistical attachments and claim fully the disciplines of the faith and a life in service to God.

Baptism is initiation into the *Khalsa*, the holy congregation. And the function of those in the Khalsa is to give themselves to single-minded meditation of the mantra, the word of God that leads to liberation.

FINDING ONE'S MANTRA THROUGH THE PREACHED WORD

For the masses of Hindus it is the experience of mantra in the form of the great epic poems like the *Ramayana* that is most common.[19] In North India the verses of Tulsidasa's *Ramayana*, the *Ramacaritmanasa*, are quoted by millions of people ranging from the scholar to the illiterate villager, in towns and villages regardless of caste distinctions. For them these remembered verses constitute their channel for hearing the divine. How do these millions, especially the illiterate, come to know not only the story but also the mantras, the verses of the poem by heart? By repeated hearing of the text being performed in a variety of forms from the *Rama Lila* folk dramas to the musical performance by folksingers and the preaching of the text by traditional scholars. The *Rama Lila* takes place as a formal drama at specified festival occasions in particular cities. But the retelling of the Rama text goes on constantly in the singing of folksingers around the village fire in the evenings and by the oral exposition of the text in *katha*, or storytelling style, by scholars. These three forms of oral transmission of the mantras or verses of the *Ramayana* are experienced by all from a very young age and result in the mantras being passed on most efficiently from generation to generation. Although other texts such as the *Mahabharata* and the *Bhagavata Purana* are also passed on in this way, in north India it is the *Ramacaritmanasa* of Tulsidasa that is by far the most popular. The katha or oral exposition of the mantras of the *Ramayana* in many ways resembles the rabbinic style of teaching in Judaism and the Western Christian tradition of exegetical preaching. Katha is done by trained professionals, *vyasa*, who preach on a sacred verse or mantra by focusing upon a very small part of it in order to bring out its meaning. Such a performer is viewed as a spiritual descendant or temporary incarnation of the original author and is privileged to speak from a vyasa-asana or seat of honor and authority in the assembly of devotees. The vyasa may be hired by a wealthy patron or group to perform for a year or more in a set public place. The more successful vyasas often become "traveling preachers" on regular circuits offering shorter periods of exposition (e.g., seven, fifteen, or thirty days) on selected passages of the text. A top vyasa may receive as much as several thousand rupees per hour for his exposition of the epic. This money may be collected as a free offering at the end of each performance. Such vyasas, today, rank among the highest paid and most famous performers in northern India.

The majority of contemporary vyasas are brahmin males who spend a great deal of time early in their careers committing all of the text to memory under the supervision of a teacher who is a successful exponent of the art. Recently a number of women have gained renown as vyasas. Lutgendorf, who interviewed a number of vyasas, reports that most described their choice of this vocation as the result of spiritual experience or a response to an inner summons to dedicate their lives to the propagation of the epic and the experience of bhakti or devotion.[20] Although printed texts and notes from teachers may be used for study or preparation, the exposition or performance itself is always extemporaneous and done without notes. A printed version of the text will always be present, and may be open or, more often, closed and ceremonially wrapped in rich cloths and garlanded with flowers on an ornate stand in front of the performer. Vyasas emphasize the importance of spontaneity and inspiration, with some even going so far as to allow audience members or patrons to select the theme or mantra for exposition. The style of exposition is such that members of the audience are actively involved—to begin with by joining the vyasa in brief kirtan or melodious chant of the name of Rama. When the vyasa begins he may often open by quoting lines from the text and pausing to allow the audience to complete the last word or phrase of the passage. The performer usually starts speaking softly and slowly with his voice gaining in strength and speed as he proceeds. A typical exposition lasts an hour, with the end of the discourse being signaled by a sudden resumption of the opening kirtan in which the audience will join with particular fervor if the exposition was good. What the vyasa aims at is not logical argument, but the creation of a devotional mood in his listeners (a *bhakti rasa*).[21]

The oral presentation and experience of the Hindi *Ramayana* has been described in some detail in an attempt to convey the flavor and vitality that preached mantras still enjoy in the Hindu tradition. It is through such oral exposition that the Hindu scriptures are transmitted from generation to generation. Such oral preaching provides for the dynamic grounding of the Hindu community in a sacred text and the powerful use of the mantras that transform human lives.

For another quite different example of finding one's mantra through preaching or interpretation let us turn to Sufism. Within Indian Islam Sufi interpretation of the Qur'an is characterized as mystical and frequently integrates elements of Greek philosophy. The distinctive Sufi method of exegesis is well represented by the Sufi Sahl at-Tustari, a Persian who lived in the ninth century.[22] Tustari's Qur'anic interpretations take the form of phrases, sentences, or brief passages, written down by his disciples, as a result of listening intently to Qur'an recitals. "The reception of Qur'an recitals and the reaction to their impact upon the Sufi's mind involve primarily the auditive energies of the Sufi and result in Sufi speech, sometimes manifested in ecstatic utterance."[23] This listening and speaking process is transposed into a written record by a disciple noting down the Sufi master's succinct statement next to a Qur'anic phrase or word. Thus the reading of a Sufi commentary requires that the eye take in both the Qur'anic word or phrase heard by the Sufi and the response uttered in his mystic speech.

Rather than a meditative or scholarly approach to the written text, the Sufi exegete allows himself to be inspired by a word or phrase from the oral text. The nature of the inspired response is indicated in the texture of Tustari's commentary where the theme of a particular item in the commentary "is usually introduced by a Qur'anic keynote (a word or a phrase of a particular verse that strikes the mind of the commentator) and is taken up as the focal point of the interpretation."[24] Such a Qur'anic keynote clearly parallels the Hindu concept of mantra and may fairly be termed as such. Qur'anic keynote mantras can be anything from historical references to theological terms or philosophical puzzles that in one way or another have managed to awaken associations in the mind of the listening Sufi. Böwering describes the mental process as follows:

> These associations establish the essential link between the *Qur'anic* keynote and the commentary. Called for by *Qur'anic* keynotes (among them certain privileged keynotes in particular), they grow out of the matrix of Tustari's world of mystical ideas (his experience about himself, God, and the world) and find their expression in a way that can be as allusive as it is concrete, and as general as it is particular. In this process a level of synthesis is achieved which makes it impossible to discern where "exegesis" ends and "eisegesis" begins.[25]

Tustari's Sufi method of interpreting the Qur'an is thus basically an encounter between the spoken keynote mantras of scripture and the matrix of his mystical ideas. This encounter, under the influence of divine inspiration, produces associations and verbal expressions which are then recorded as the written commentary. For the Sufi these keynote mantras are not studied as a text but are heard by men experienced in listening attentively to Qur'anic recital and intent on hearing God, the actual speaker of the Qur'anic word. The keynote psychologically and spiritually functions to help the Sufi break through to God. This special Qur'anic word or mantra takes the Sufi beyond its outer form and sound to a direct revelation of God.

MANTRA IN THE LIVES OF NORTH AMERICAN SUFIS

Diana L. Eck reminds us that Sufism, the "interior path of spiritual life, is not a separate sect of Islam, but suffused through the entire tradition."[26] Various scholars of Islam have noted the periodic tension between those who have followed the Sufi path and other orthodox Muslims, tensions that are often reflected in the relationship between various mystics and orthodox Muslims who cast a wary eye toward mystics, fearing they may cross the traditional boundaries of the faith. In my own field research work in the Muslim communities in Alberta, Canada, I met Imam Ahmed al-Sharkawy twenty-five years ago when he was serving the mosque in Lac La Biche, Alberta, where a group of Lebanese fur traders had settled early in the twentieth century. Our initial conversation quickly turned to the gifts of the Sufi tradition, and he spoke of his journey to this interior path while he was studying at Al-Azhar University in Cairo and how his knowledge and practice of Sufism, particularly the discipline of the dhikr, grew while serving Muslim communities in India. He spoke of coming to Canada and his struggle to inculcate in the local Muslim community both the insights of Sufism on divine love and an understanding of how these stand at the very center of the daily prayer. Imam al-Sharkawy faced considerable resistance to his teaching about Sufism. In the twenty-five years since our first meeting that resistance has turned to acceptance and appreciation for many birthright Muslims, and Sufism has come to be prized beyond the traditional boundary of the community.

This shift, typical of North America, came about in two ways. The growing diversity of Muslims immigrating to North America meant some of them had intimate links to Sufi practice in Syria, Turkey, Egypt, India, and Africa. Also in the North American context many Sufi movements developed that have captured the imaginations and hearts of women and men who grew up in Christian, Jewish, and secular homes. Many in this latter group of spiritual refugees adopted one or another of the spiritual disciplines of Sufism, as they sought to satisfy their thirst for meaning. They came to Sufism out of a desire for a spiritual discipline they understood to be free of dogma, a discipline that encouraged the experience of the divine in personal terms. Over several decades, as they grew in the discipline and knowledge of Sufism, they came to appreciate Islamic tradition and its teaching about the human journey to the remembrance of God, the pathways of harmony, and the gratuitous nature of the cosmos.

Sufi Movements in North America

Early in the twentieth century a young Indian mystic and musician traveled to Europe and America performing Indian music and teaching what he called "the Sufi message of spiritual liberty." Pir-o-Murshid Inayat Khan (1882–1927) was an initiate of the Chishti Sufi Order[27] and from the time of his arrival in America in 1910 to his death in 1927 he presented concerts and lectures emphasizing the unity of religions and the unifying power of love. While it is obvious that the Islamic roots and center of Sufism informed and shaped his work, many women and men who were attracted to him and his teaching saw this new gospel as not specifically tied to Islam. He left a large body of literature and two fledgling groups: the Sufi Order of the West and the Sufi Movement. The numerous Sufi organizations found in many North American cities today are their descendants.[28]

Various members of Pir-o-Murshid Inayat Khan's family continued his work and left a marked influence on the contemporary shape of Sufism, particularly among converts. His son, Hidayat Inayat Khan, has taught throughout North America and Europe. In 1979 the Sufi Movement in Canada worked with him to establish an annual summer camp at Lake O'Hara in Yoho National Park, near Lake Louise in the Canadian Rocky Mountains. Here, on what he often called the "sacred Sufi hill" in the heart of the natural temple of the mountains, "Hidayat transmits to the contemporary seeker, the essential ideas of his father's message, which is

FIGURE 3.4 Hidayat Inayat Khan, Pir-o-Murshid (first teacher) of the Sufi Movement International, leading the prayers, with movements, at Lake O'Hara. COURTESY DAVID MURRAY

an ancient message of Divine Wisdom hidden in every heart."[29] At the core of his message is the path of remembrance, the sung *dhikr* (Arabic, "remembrance, mention"; also transliterated *zikar*), a form of mantra best known in the West through its central place in Sufi spiritual discipline.[30]

Dhikr, the Pathway to Spiritual Liberty

The scholarship on dhikr in the Western languages has often emphasized the set of bodily movements employed by various Sufi groups as a way of anchoring the powers of concentration and neglected the importance of

FIGURE 3.5 A group of Sufis by Lake O'Hara using movements with the element practices. In this case the hand gesture is for the element earth. COURTESY CAROLE HARMON

this concept in the Qur'an. Dhikr and terms deriving from it are used 270 times in the Qur'an and the sung dhikr taught to North Americans by Hidayat Inayat Khan is a play on the *shahadah* (creedal statement), the opening line of the First Pillar of Islam: "La ilaha illa Allah" ("There is no god but God"). Hidayat Inayat Khan notes that

> Zikar is the process of repeating the sacred words as a meditation, that the meaning of the words may be impressed on the entire self. The Vedanta has called this process "Mantra Yog" or "Jap." The Sufis have in all ages given great importance to this, for it is not only the thought but also the vibration of the sacred words combined with the motion of the body which makes perfect concentration. For a sincere disciple it does not take more than six weeks to discover its effect upon the self. It is wonderful in its power of giving inner realization.[31]

Various Sufi masters, including Abu Hamid al-Ghazali (1058–1111), Ibn al-'Arabi (1165–1240), and Jalal al Din Rumi (1207–1273), taught that the remembrance of God brought about a recovery of primordial human nature. Since human nature is a divine image, its recovery calls forth all the perfections latent within the human being. These perfections ultimately belong to God, the one true being, and this remembrance is the sign of the fully realized human person. "When one pursues the dhikr and persists in it, the attachment of the spirit to other than God will be gradually severed by the scissors of *la ila ha*, and the beauty of the monarch of *illa Allah* will be manifest and emerge from the veil of might."[32] Rumi, the most popular Muslim mystic in the West, saw in the passion of love the human being seeking to remember the divine. "Love" he said, "is that flame which, when it blazes up, burns away everything except the beloved. It drives home the sword of *la ilaha* in order to slay other than God."[33]

Hidayat Inayat Khan's teaching on the singing dhikr, popular among North American Sufis, brings together the sung word, breathing and bodily movement using a slightly modified form of the shahadah. The four stages of preparation for entering into the dhikr begin by recalling that one's body is not one's own but is the temple of God. The disciple, ideally seated in the yoga position, accompanies this "remembrance" by drawing

FIGURE 3.6 Practicing the *movements to accompany a prayer on the jetty on* Lake O'Hara. COURTESY DAVID MURRAY

his or her right hand across the chest and tracing a vertical line from the forehead downwards identifying the "Prana channel along which the Divine Presence is invited into the temple of one's heart."[34] The second stage invites one to visualize standing outside oneself, tracing the same lines as before but concluding with the palm of the hand turned upward. Stage three repeats this gesture, not with the movement of the arm and hand, but mentally in one's mind's eye and with a relaxed and gentle movement of the head. The final stage of preparation is done as a faqir, a simple disciple under the guidance of a master, and here the same movement is joined to the rhythm of one's breathing and the mental recitation of the dhikr: "La El La Ha, El Allah Hu" ("God alone exists, none exists save He"). The words "la el la ha" are combined with breathing out and the inhaling of breath accompanies the words "el Allah hu." Breathing out is a surrender through which the seeker begins to set aside the illusions that color one's sense of oneself and of the world. Breathing in affirms the divine presence in all that is.

The singing dhikr is at once the deepest song of the human heart and, at its inception, an opening and call for God to enter what Hidayat Inayat Khan repeatedly calls "the temple of my heart." Like so many mantras in the religions of India, it is a love song expressing the opening of the heart to the divine. Through the dhikr each disciple is pleading, over and over again in the daily chant, for the Divine Beloved to be present:

> There is the idea of a duality here, the Beloved and my heart, so we haven't yet reached the final ideal of the Zikar. Zikar one is the love song to the Beloved, and Zikar two is an appeal for the Divine Presence to come into the temple of the heart. Zikar three is again one step further; God is responding, God is calling, saying: "But I am there in your heart; you did not see me but I was always there."[35]

Inayat Khan teaches that this simple mantra, with its seven words drawn from the heart of Islam, contains the seed of these three spiritual steps. They lead one to the ultimate meaning and purpose of the dhikr, which he identifies as step four. It is here the seeker realizes that there is only the Beloved, only God, and in the face of God the reality of what he calls the dualism of the Beloved and the human heart fades entirely: "The Beloved is there but the Lover is no longer there; there is only Beloved and Love."[36] Inayat Khan stands in a long line of Sufis, chief among them being the celebrated mystic and saint of Baghdad, Rabi'ah al-'Adawiyah (717–801) who taught that union with God could be achieved through love alone. It was her experience of this fourth step, where the discipline of the dhikr completed its work, that led her to say, "O God, if I worship thee for fear of Hell, burn me in Hell, and if I worship thee in hope of Paradise, exclude me from Paradise; but if I worship thee for thy own sake, grudge me not thy everlasting beauty."[37]

The purpose of dhikr is not to make one a spiritual person or lead one to the annihilation of the ego. It is, as the word implies, a form of remembrance of the divine presence. As many Sufis have pointed out, it only makes sense to use this practice if it leads one to forget about one's own ego and to forget that one wants to forget. This discipline of remembrance of the divine matures in the disciples and nurtures the capacity of the dis-

FIGURE 3.7 Nirtan Carole-Ann Sokoloff, Sufi songwriter and dance leader, at Lake O'Hara Lodge jetty practicing her music. COURTESY CAROLE HARMON

ciples to forget about themselves in the midst of daily life. When this occurs, the disciple is suddenly grasped by the divine presence. Inayat Khan, standing in the golden stream of the tradition of mantra in India, teaches that it is

> during our daily occupations or while resting, that universal sound resounds at unexpected occasions, as a result of which we become lost in the eternal "Hu." The sound of all the planets, the sound of the universe, in fact the only sound there is. The sound of the Divine Presence. If the word "sacred" ever had a definition, it would be just this: to forget that we wanted to forget ourselves, our egos. And all of a sudden we are confronted with the Divine Presence. Without any want, without any desire . . . and that is why, "not to be is to be." Because when one has no more desire, no more want, one is at-one with the Divine Presence.[38]

MANTRA IN THE LIVES OF NORTH AMERICAN SIKHS

Sikh tradition, along with the various other religions of India, has come to make its home in North America through the immigration and settlement of its faithful over the better part of the last century. Just as Hindu, Buddhist, and Muslim gurus and teachers have come to the West, so too have various Sikh teachers come to encourage the interested faithful and to call men and women alienated from their Jewish, Christian, and secular sources of meaning to the practice of mantra rooted in the teaching of Guru Nanak. Perhaps none has had a greater impact on the lives of converts in North America than Yogi Bhajan, who developed the 3HO Foundation (Healthy, Happy, Holy Organization).

Yogi Bhajan was born Siri Singh Sahib Harbhajan Khalsa on August 26, 1929, in Kot Harkarn in Pakistan. His father was a physician and landowner in the region and he encouraged his young son to study with Sant Hazara Singh. When Yogi Bhajan was sixteen, Hazara Singh declared him a master of Kundalini yoga. The young master journeyed to various ashrams in the Himalayas, meeting many other masters of Kundalini and deepening his studies. In his early formative period he also served for a time at the Golden Temple in Amritsar, the seat of Sikh tradition.

Yogi Bhajan founded the 3HO Foundation in 1969 and it now operates more than three hundred centers of learning in thirty-five countries. The foundation has given a modern shape to the ancient science of Kundalini yoga by offering methods for the perfection of the individual through physical exercise, breath control, and meditation that restores balance to the physical, mental, and spiritual life. His emphasis on health offers to improve all aspects of the body from the respiratory and circulatory systems to the immune system, and many devotees credit it with restoring youthful vigor. Its emphasis on happiness is rooted in restoring the power of concentration and restoring tranquility to one's inner life. The third emphasis of Yogi Bhajan's work has been on holiness, the culmination of human life restoring the individual's experience of unity with the infinite and a sense of being at home in the universe. All three of these areas are targeted to a generation of women and men who had become alienated and confused through the use of drugs and other forms of behavior leading them out of the fullness of life. The literature of the 3HO Foundation brings together Kundalini and Sikh meditation techniques and builds on the holistic health movements common in America since the nineteenth century as well as more recent movements accenting a positive mental attitude and each individual's right to a materially successful life.[39] A central, if not the central, mantra taught by Yogi Bhajan is also the central mantra in Sikh tradition, the one that animates the Sikh baptism ritual and washes over virtually every Sikh service. What distinguishes Yogi Bhajan's teaching of this mantra from its common use in Sikh discipline is his recommended gestures and breathing exercise that accompany the words as well as the use of this mantra for extended periods of time by each devotee throughout the day.

"*Wha-Hay Guroo*," the Mantra of Mantras

The *wha-hay guroo* (literally an expression of astonishment at the illumination of the guru) mantra, according to Yogi Bhajan, has great transformative powers capable of rebuilding the personal identity of the disciple, purifying the subconscious of the disciple's impulses, and restoring balance to a troubled body, mind, and spirit. It works to restore health, happiness, and holiness even for those who have come close to squandering their life and being. Yogi Bhajan says that of all the forms of yoga and mantra, including Kundalini yoga, this mantra is of the highest order:

> This meditation cuts through all darkness. It will give you a new start. It is the simplest *kriya* (action) but at the same time the hardest. It cuts through all barriers of the neurotic and psychotic inside-nature. When a person is in a very bad state, techniques imposed from the outside will not work. The pressure has to be stimulated from within. The tragedy of life is when the subconscious releases garbage into the conscious mind. This *kriya* invokes the Kundalini to give you the necessary vitality and intuition to combat the negative effects of the subconscious mind.[40]

Yogi Bhajan's instruction combines the use of the Sikh mantra with Kundalini yoga exercises. The person meditating is to sit in an easy position, on the floor with legs crossed in the manner of a yogi, if possible. First the person blocks the right nostril with the right thumb and inhales slowly and deeply through the left nostril, suspends breathing and holds the breath while mentally chanting the mantra *wha-hay guroo* sixteen times. The chant is slow and deliberate and with each of the three notes of the mantra—*wha, hay, guroo*—the person pumps the navel point three times for a total of 48 unbroken pumps. Slowly and deliberately the person repeats this sixteen times. Then the exercise, the prayer, is repeated by blocking the right nostril in the same manner. Yogi Bhajan recommends this exercise be done initially for 5 minutes and then for 11 or 31 minutes. When one becomes a master practitioner the mantra session is extended to 62 minutes and finally to 150 minutes a day.

In his book *The Teachings of Yogi Bhajan*, this master of the Sikh mantra provides the reader with 783 short, cryptic "sentences," each of which is a meditation in itself. In the preface he tells us that this book contains "the hidden science of Nadh, the science of eternal sound . . . spoken from the consciousness of a Mahan Tantric, for which privilege I, as a human being in this time and space, am grateful to God and Guru Ram Das."[41] He wrote this book for a North American audience, drawing in an eclectic way on Christian texts, arguing for the universal character of the mantra and its power to heal those who have lost their way in life and are in danger of losing themselves. He speaks of the integrity of the person over against doctrines of the degradation of human nature, calls those who suffer physically to a pathway of recovery, and gives an apology for moral uprightness and the value of committed relationships between men and women. He speaks directly to the drug culture and the libertine models of life popularized in the 1960s and holds out to the individual the opportunity to experience the infinite and come to rest in God: "A polluted mind deludes one's sense of self, and sometimes the sense of self is so deluded that self-respect is lost. When self-respect is lost, grace is lost; when grace is lost, the word is lost; when the word is lost, then sacrifice is lost. Sacrifice can only happen when you know the word."[42] His teaching and his method is to liberate the person in the midst of the affairs of life, a teaching at the center of Sikh tradition since Guru Nanak. Meditation is the pathway to liberation since "meditation is the creative control of the self where the Infinite can talk to you."[43] All human beings are "habit-free beings" in their nature but "slowly develop habits" and increasingly justify these habits despite their destructive nature. The practice of the mantra restores the mind to its original condition and in so doing the human being comes to liberation:

> O mind, when you were not born you were with Infinity. You were given this finite body to realize the Infinity in the finite and you will leave this body to go to the Infinity again. O mind, again you will be with Infinity, so why are you worried? If God has given you grace, He has given you grace. When you were a child you were taken care of through certain adverse circumstances and certain favorable circumstances. But through all the circumstances, He took care of you and brought you to the shore of maturity. Now, when you are mature, why do you worry?[44]

FINDING ONE'S MANTRA THROUGH THE SINGING OF MANTRAS

The chanted mantra often seems to increase in its power to evoke the divine when it is sung. The major Indian religions have devised different techniques for doing this, and we will sample some of them. The singing of mantras as hymns or *kirtans* is common to Hindus and Sikhs. A number of Hindu movements rely primarily on the sung mantra as a way to release or moksa. Sikhs have developed a unique way of "singing" their scripture from the pulpit, and the Tibetan Buddhists have created a special technique for chanting OM MANI PADME HUM with each monk singing the full D-major chord. Let us examine these in turn.

The Sung Mantra as a Way to Release

Throughout much of popular Hinduism a rich tradition of singing kirtan to the god or goddess of one's heart flourishes. It is done in homes and temples and in the streets on festive occasions.[45]

As mentioned above in our discussion of ISKCON, a bhakti tradition developing from the sixteenth-century reformer and ecstatic mystic Caitanya (1486–1533) understands the sung mantra as a love song to Lord Krishna. In that singing a purification takes place. All karmas that cloud the soul's longing for union with God are burned up in the passionate expression of the devotee's love mantra for Lord Krishna.

The union of the soul with Krishna moves from longing to a meeting in the "trysting place, full of all desired bliss." Lover and beloved become one in ecstatic song.

Krishna is known primarily as a lover. Radha, a cowgirl, was the chief object of his affection. The *Gita Govinda*, written in the twelfth century by Jayadeva, expresses the intensity of their love.

> He has gone into the trysting-place, full of all desired bliss,
> O you with the lovely hips delay no more
> O go forth now and seek him out, him the master of your heart,
> O go forth now and seek him out, him the master of your heart,
> him endowed with passion's lovely form.[46]

The songs and stories about Radha and Krishna are songs about the longing of love, about moments of consummation and bliss and longing again. Just so does the devotee long for union with the divine, find it momentarily, and lose it again amidst the distractions and desires of everyday life.

Caitanya went on pilgrimage to do sacramental service for his recently deceased wife. He was serving a lost love for a human being and in this service to love found himself opened to the love of Krishna whose stories and songs were focused on longing and loving union. He became a lover of Krishna and would wander through the streets and roads singing his love mantra to Krishna. The people of his home region, Nadia, saw him as transformed, as having become Radha the lover of Krishna. His ecstasy moved from longing for the beloved Krishna to periods of bliss in which he was said to embody the union of lover and beloved. Devotees gathered around him, and he taught them the love mantra.

The faith of Krishna-Caitanya teaches that Brahman is manifest in the quintessential way in Krishna. All human beings emanate from the divine source. They are paradoxically different and yet not different from God. The soul can be brought only by divine mercy (krpa) to realize its true nature as the servant of Krishna. Caitanya saw the time in which he lived as a decadent age (*kaliyuga*) in which people needed divine help to fulfill their religious duties and find release. He offered a simple way for souls to be delivered from bondage and spiritual ignorance. All a devotee need do is identify with one of Krishna's parents, companions, or lovers. Caitanya had a passionate love for Krishna and identified so deeply with the Lord's divine mistress Radha that he was seen to embody the presence of both Krishna and Radha.

The Sikh Experience of the Guru Granth Sahib as Sung Mantras

Earlier in this chapter we said that one finds one's mantra through the guru. This Hindu practice has been given interesting development by the Sikhs. For them the whole of their scripture is taken to be the divine guru—to be consulted on a daily basis for guidance as well as during congregational worship. The mantras or verses of the hymns that comprise the Sikh scripture, the Guru Granth Sahib, have been written down in book form. It is from the written copy in the village gurdwara or temple that most Sikhs in India memorize their prayers and hymns. Some may also be fortunate to have a copy in their home. The presence of the written mantras in the gurdwara and home also provides what a living guru would provide—the physical manifestation of the divine. But the words of the Guru Granth Sahib function quite differently from the words of ordinary books or even of other scriptures. In Sikh devotion the words of the mantras or verses fulfill the same function as that of a musical score in relation to performed music. Just as the written music has no value until it is performed, so the written text of the Guru Granth Sahib has spiritual power only as it is sung. This is evident in the very structure of the written text. It is poetry, and at the top of each hymn the name of the raga and rhythm to be used in its singing are clearly stated. This is why the devotional experience of scripture cannot be had from translations—just as it is impossible to translate a Bach fugue into some other form. As is the case with the learning of music, if it is learned by heart in childhood it will never be forgotten. One may not bother with it for awhile, but it will always be there in the unconscious and later in life one will likely come back to it. But if music is not learned in childhood, it is very difficult to learn it (especially by heart) later in life. As kirtan or sung mantras, the Sikh experience of scripture is very similar. Its music and poetry, when learned in youth, has a formative influence throughout life. Once learned, the constant singing and chanting of the mantras is described by one devotee as "vibrating into you . . . clearing and opening your mind to God's grace."[47] Ultimately it enables one to "dwell within the house of the *Guru's* Word." In village India, where most adult Sikhs now living in Europe and North America grew up, this kind of devotional immersing of oneself in scripture happened quite naturally and without great self-effort.

> I knew people in the village where I grew up as a child . . . those people had a very simple life. You get up in the morning and do prayers (together as a family or community) and then go and do your work. In the evening you sit and there would be prayers and a wiseman or priest who would interpret the *gurbani* (scripture), and people would sit there for two or three hours with no temptations to get away from it.[48]

In this rural traditional environment, with no television, radio, or other modern distractions, the divine music of the Guru Granth Sahib surrounded one and was naturally absorbed into one's consciousness.

The Singing of Mantras in Tibetan Buddhism

Tibetan Buddhists are now found in several centers in northern India. They hold that music, and singing the scriptures in particular, prepares the mind for enlightenment.[49] Consequently, choral chant with or without instrumental accompaniment predominates in the five daily assemblies of monks in the monastery shrine hall.

Characteristically, the monks—through chant—offer an invitation to the deity to be present in the place of worship, offer ritual service to the

FIGURE 3.8 A group of Sikh musicians perform the kirtan sung mantras and sacred hymns in the gurdwara. PHOTOGRAPH AARON GOOS; COURTESY OF THE FOLKLIFE PROGRAM, PROVINCIAL MUSEUM OF ALBERTA

deity, and offer hymns of thanksgiving and praise to the Buddha and bodhisattvas. This is done sitting cross-legged in paired rows facing each other and directed by a chant leader (*dbumdza*). The texts are drawn mostly from the two sacred scriptures known as Bka-gyur and Bstan-gyur.

Two monasteries of the Dge-lungs-pa order in Tibet cultivated a special chant technique that is current in the Tibetan communities in India. The chanting of the Buddhist mantra OM MANI PADME HUM is accompanied with a set of ritual gestures that act out the meaning of the mantra. Thus the monks feel and act the mantra as well as say it. And the saying of it is not simple speaking but a chanting that involves the "singing" of a D-major chord by each monk individually. Through changes in intonation, pitch, loudness, and (most remarkably) overtone mixtures, each monk is perceived actually to chant D-F#-A simultaneously.

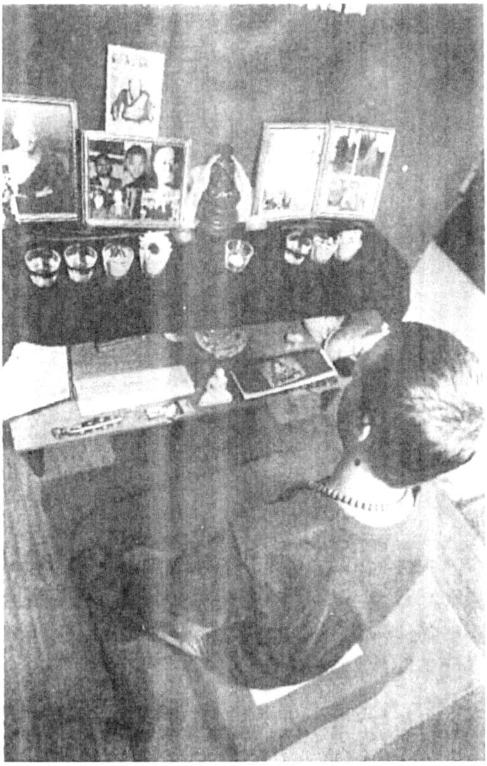

FIGURE 3.9 A young Canadian practitioner of Tibetan forms of mantra meditation. PHOTOGRAPH AARON GOOS; COURTESY OF THE FOLKLIFE PROGRAM, PROVINCIAL MUSEUM OF ALBERTA

This singing of two pitches, a deep fundamental pitch and a clear harmonic pitch, results in an extraordinary choral effect and is said to evoke in the singer and hearer a sense of the interdependence of the universe. This recognition of the interdependence of all things is exactly what the Buddha's enlightenment experience made clear. That which is deep within and fundamental to the self rings clear with cosmic harmonies. The chant is experienced by the chanters (and by the listeners) as being more powerful than a mere saying of the mantras. The singing of the syllables makes present the divine reality they symbolize.

Singing Mantras in a Christian Tradition

Groups of Tibetan monks frequently tour America offering such performances of sung chant to the general public. In all our examples of sung mantra in India we have glimpsed the power of mantra to transform the lives of the devotees. Gregorian chant, which for centuries was the staple of Western liturgical music, is a Christian example that can heighten our appreciation of how chant influences the inner life and liberates the person. Or it may be that our study of Indian mantra singing will open the way to a better understanding of Gregorian chant.

Rembert Herbert in a lovely essay has sketched the effect of Gregorian chant on the singer.[50] He draws on his experience with a Schola Cantorum and on a careful reading of Gregory the Great from whom Gregorian chant takes its name.

What is practiced by the contemplative tradition, and the understanding of the inner life within that tradition, are made available by Gregorian chant to the singer. The quiet repetitive character of the music invites the instability of one's mind and heart, emotional attachments and images of oneself, the whole inner cacophany to bubble to the surface. These attachments, claimed by the unconscious as central to one's character, clamor for attention and in that clamor dull one's attentiveness to the real self.

The singer has to struggle against this inner clamor, against these "aimless wanderings" of the mind—karmas as the Indian tradition would call them. It is through resisting the inner clamor that the ability to listen to the music, listen to the harmonies is developed. As listening deepens, singing, music, and text gradually gain prominence and, as Herbert puts it,

> one finds that a transparency appears in the sound of the group, so that impulses or inflections of meaning can move through the choir almost instantaneously. In this way it becomes possible for the choir (and each singer), through its singing, to touch the text with a new intimacy and immediacy.[51]

This prepares, as Gregory the Great puts it, "a way to the heart for almighty God."[52] After singing Gregorian chant for some time, the inner cacophony is no longer central. One begins to hear the text and its meaning. There is a new soundscape within oneself, shaped by the chant.

When chant takes hold in this manner, the meaning of the sacred text and the silence in the music, the action of speaking and the contemplation of listening come into balance. This attention to sound and silence is key. It cultivates a quiet attentiveness in the singer, an attentiveness that does not attach itself to the wanderings of the mind, to the vagaries of the heart, to desires born of memory or imagination.

Origen compares the soul at this moment, when the balance between the active speaking and contemplative listening comes to rest at the center of the self, with the divine lover in the Song of Songs, "leaping upon the mountain, skipping over the hills." We saw earlier that for Caitanya the soul is the divine lover, prepared by the sung mantra for union with God. The union with God comes in the attentiveness induced by the chant and not through imagination or memory at play.

Mantra in Christian Dialogue with Indian Masters

The story of the Christian encounter with the religious world of India runs like a golden strand from the time of the apostle Thomas. According to popular belief in South India, he landed on the Malabar coast in 52 C.E., followed twenty years later by his martyrdom on the east coast at Madras (Chinnai).[53] The Thomas (Syriac) Christians in Kerala trace their origins to "doubting Thomas" and this Church maintained contacts with churches in Edessa, Chaldea, Persia, and Mesopotamia through two millennia, although it was little known in the Christian West. French Dominicans and Franciscans reached India in 1321 and the Portuguese arrived with Vasco da Gama in 1498, bringing traders, their own colonial administration, a bevy of Franciscan friars, and Latin Christianity to Goa. In the accounts by these early Franciscans we read of their surprise to learn that the Syrian Christian tradition had flourished south of them since apostolic times. With the arrival of St. Francis Xavier in 1542, the Jesuit mission took hold and his compelling preaching led to many baptisms and deepened Roman Catholic efforts to Latinize the Thomas Christians.

Missionaries are often interested in local religious life, and it was no different in this case. The Hindu monastic and mystical tradition associated with the forest dwellers (*rsis*) and the spiritual discipline of the sannyasa, with their asceticism and meditation to attain enlightenment and union with the divine in the "cave of the heart" as well as the place of the guru, attracted the attention of many, including Robert de Nobili, S.J. (1577–1656). His encounter with Hindu masters led de Nobili to vow to live as a sannyasi, follow a rigorous regime of fasting, dress as a Brahmin, and pray in a Hindu style. Through his study of Tamil and Sanskrit and his reading of the Vedas he developed theological terms suitable, he argued, for the Indian context of Christianity. De Nobili has been called the "father of Christian sannyasa." Two hundred years later three Syro-Malabar priests established the Carmelites of Mary Immaculate (C.M.I.) in 1831, bringing together sannyasic elements, Indian methods of contemplation and spiritual guidance, and Western Christian notions of community service in a monastic community. Brahmabandhab Upadjyay (1861–1907), a Brahmin convert to Catholicism, became a sannyasi in 1894, deepening the Christian monastic conversation with the Vedas. He also wrote on the Trinity as a form of *Saccidananda* (*Sat-Cit-Ananda*), the divine name. He established a Catholic monastery, Kasthalic Matha. Orthodox Syrian Christians established the Bethany ashram in 1918. Ashrams founded by Mahatma Gandhi (1869–1948) inspired the founding of Christukula in Tamil Nadu and Christa Seva Sangha in Puna, the first Protestant ashrams.

In the twentieth century French and English Benedictines, along with several Americans, brought the influence of Indian spiritual discipline and its nurturing institutions, the mantra and monastic communities, to engender the recovery of contemplation within the Christian community in Indian and North American religious life.

In 1947 the Benedictine monk Henri Le Saux (1910–1973) began corresponding with a confrere in India, Jules Monchanin (1895–1957). Monchanin had gone to India with the express purpose of establishing a Christian contemplative monastic community.[54] Henri Le Saux joined him a year later and in 1950 they founded Saccidananda Ashram, or Shantivanam, in the village of Tannirpalli in Tamil Nadu near the city of Trichy.

Here they lived in a simple and primitive way, following the typical pattern of the Hindu renunciate. Le Saux came to be called Abhishktananda, commonly translated as "the Bliss of the Anointed One" or the "Bliss of Christ."

Abhishktananda and Monchanin traveled to Arunachala to be in the presence of one of modern India's greatest saints, Ramana Maharshi (1879–1950). Maharshi was a rare silent seer, a *muni.* Like the great *rsis* of antiquity, he incarnated the stillness that forms the heart of Indian mysticism within the pure nondualist, *advaitin* tradition. After Maharshi's death the caves at Arunachala became Abhishktananda's spiritual home and he pursued inner experience that took him deep into *advaita,* pure nondual (unitive) awareness. His book shows his work reconciling Christian faith and mysticism with his experience of meeting Maharshi and reorienting his thinking around the experience of advaita.[55]

Bede Griffiths (1907–1993) wrote in *The Golden String* (1954), a title taken from William Blake's poem "Heaven's Gate," of his journey from agnosticism to Catholicism and the monastic life in a Benedictine community. After twenty-five years in English monasteries during which his interest in the art of prayer and contemplation flourished, he accepted an invitation from an Indian monk, Father Benedict Alapatt, to come to India and establish a Benedictine community. He wrote to a friend, "I am going out to India to seek the other half of my soul," the intuitive, feminine, mystical dimensions of being. His first attempt to establish a Benedictine community failed. In 1958 he joined Father Francis Mahieu, a Belgian Cistercian, and founded Kurisumala Ashram in Kerala, where Griffiths served as novice master, professor, and guest master for a decade. In the mid 1960s, when Abhishktananda was moving to the solitary life and longed to withdraw from Shantivanam Ashram, he asked Kurisumala Ashram to take over the responsibilities for Shantivanam. Griffiths was sent as the new superior to Shantivanam in 1968, giving Abhishktananda the opportunity to withdraw to his hermitage at Uttakashi in the Himalayas, where he died in December 1973.

Bede Griffiths, perhaps the most articulate and prolific writer on Christian mantra, provided stable and visionary leadership for the community of the Shantivanam Ashram from 1968 to his death in 1993. This ashram became an important monastic presence drawing many Christians and others who were seeking a formation in contemplative prayer. Griffiths entered the Camaldolese Benedictine congregation in 1980 and brought Shantivanam into this wing of Catholic monastic institutions. He was encouraged by the teachings of the Second Vatican Council (1962–1965), culminating in the document *Nostra Aetate*, "Declaration on the Relation of the Church to Non-Christian Religions."[56] In article 2 of this document the Fathers of the Council wrote, "In Hinduism men contemplate the divine mystery and express it through an unspent fruitfulness of myths and through searching philosophical inquiry. They seek release from the anguish of our condition through ascetical practices or deep meditation or a loving, trusting flight toward God." Griffiths took encouragement from the council to engage in a deep and respectful dialogue with Hinduism and Buddhism and led Shantivanam Ashram on a path that has grown to reflect the enculturation of Hindu thought and practice.

The Shantivanam Ashram is dedicated to the Holy Trinity and is a "hybrid of Catholic monastic life and Hindu *sannyasa*."[57] Griffiths, both as a result of his personal quest and as a son of the Church, saw his task as engaging in a deep and sustained dialogue with the spiritual treasures of India while standing on and drawing from the sources of meaning within the Catholic tradition that had initially ignited his conversion and entry into monasticism. The personalist theological discourse that had influenced his theological education as a young man,[58] and the experience and writing of the Spanish mystics, with their singular emphasis on divine love, reshaped his inner life as well as his concern for the deepening of the gospel of love within the Catholic community. In a letter he wrote to Wayne Teasdale, three years before his death, Griffiths said, "I find myself in the Void (the emptiness, or *shunyata* of the Buddhists), but the Void is totally saturated with love."[59]

The fourth example of a twentieth-century monastic who engaged in dialogue with the tradition of mantra in India and played an important role in the recovery of contemplative prayer for Christians in North America and elsewhere is Dom John Main, OSB (1926–1982).[60] While stationed in the Far East with the British Colonial Service, Main, in a routine visit on behalf of the government, visited Swami Satyananda, a Hindu master of meditation.[61] He told Satyananda of his difficulty in praying and through a series of conversations was led into the practice of mantra. On his return to the United Kingdom, Main taught international law briefly at Trinity College, Dublin, continuing his daily meditation practice. He was accepted into the order of St. Benedict at Ealing Abbey in 1959, with the express desire to deepen his meditation. As a novice he was forbidden to use this method of meditation and told it was not part of the Christian tradition. This was a period of considerable struggle for the young Main, but he accepted responsibility for his vow of obedience and refrained from the practice, giving himself to the liturgical life of the congregation and praying the monastic office. Main was sent to be headmaster of St. Anselm's Abbey School in Washington, DC, and tells how, in 1970, a troubled young man consulted him on prayer. This young man was quite unfamiliar with Christian monastic practice. Main recommended he read the Benedictine classic by Augustine Baker, *Holy Wisdom*, and that he come again to discuss the book.[62] Main was so taken by the impact of this book on the young man that he reread it, only to discover again Baker's remarkable description of the place of silence at the center of contemplative prayer. Now a full-fledged monk and recalled to Ealing Abbey in 1974, he began to research the sources of the mantra in the Benedictine tradition back through Baker and the twelfth-century Cistercian writers to the Patristic Fathers and the fourth-century desert monk John Cassian.[63] Augustine Baker reminded Main of the reliance St. Benedict, the founder of the Benedictine order, had on Cassian's *Conferences*.

Main reconciled his experience studying meditation with Satyananda with the Benedictine tradition, returned to his meditation practice, and began to speak to his fellow monks about contemplative prayer and the place of silence in the life of Christians. A charismatic figure, Main invited lay people to form a meditation group around Ealing and began teaching them the art of contemplative prayer. In 1977 he was invited by the archbishop of Montreal to found a Benedictine community focused on teaching Christian meditation. He was accompanied by his fellow monk, Lawrence Freeman, and they founded the Benedictine Priory of Montreal. Since the Second Vatican Council had encouraged experiments in monastic life and the relationship of monasteries to lay communities, Main and Freeman developed an associated community of lay women and men, single and married, to live alongside the priory. Through this lay association they invited others to meet weekly for meditation and encouraged them to adopt the discipline of meditating twice daily. The work grew into the World Community for Christian Meditation, which has come to span the world with its retreats, conferences, and publications.[64]

Mantra and the Recovery of Contemplative Prayer in Christianity

John Main's three conferences given at Gethsemani Abbey in November 1976 are perhaps as fine a way as any for us to understand mantra and the recovery of contemplative prayer within the Western Christian tradition.[65] He opened his first talk by reflecting on his teacher, Swami Satyananda, who had a temple just outside Kuala Lumpur, Malaya. Main had come on business as a member of the British Colonial Service and describes how, when the business was finished, the swami asked him if he was religious and if he meditated. Main spoke about his Catholic faith and described briefly the Ignatian method of meditation that he had been trying to use in recent years.[66] After a moment of silence the swami talked of his own very different meditation and said that its aim was to grow in "awareness of the Spirit of the universe who dwells in our hearts." He quoted the Upanisads: "He contains all things, all works and desires and all perfumes and tastes. And he enfolds the whole universe and, in silence, is loving to all. This is the Spirit that is in my heart. This is Brahman."[67]

The swami's quiet, peaceful character and devotion touched the young colonial officer and he asked to be accepted as a pupil in order to learn how to meditate in this way. He was assured that this form of meditation was simple and that, if Main would come once a week to meditate together, he would try to teach him. Main recalled Swami Satyananda's words to him when they met a week later:

> To meditate you must become silent. You must be still. And you must concentrate. In our tradition we know one way in which you can arrive

> at that stillness, that concentration. We use a "word" that we call a "mantra." To meditate, what you must do is to choose this word and then repeat it, faithfully, lovingly and continually. That is all there is to meditation. I really have nothing else to tell you. And now we will meditate.[68]

Over the next eighteen months Main returned every week to sit with this holy man of God and meditate with him for half an hour. Following each session Satyananda would teach him about mantra and the pathway to union with God. He began to meditate for half an hour early each morning and again in the evening, seeking to root the mantra in his heart and to be free from all other thoughts, words, and imaginings. You are seeking that state of consciousness, Swami Satyananda told him, in which the only sound in your heart and mind

> will be the sound of your mantra, your word. The mantra is like a harmonic. And as we sound this harmonic within ourselves we begin to build up a resonance. That resonance, then leads us forward to our own wholeness. . . . We begin to experience the deep unity we all possess in our own being. And then the harmonic begins to build up a resonance between you and all creation and all creation and a unity between you and your Creator.[69]

Main went on to describe how, when he became a monk, he was discouraged from continuing this form of prayer and, in obedience as a Benedictine novice, he took up the new method, the "prayer of acts," which is a half hour spent in acts of adoration, contrition, thanksgiving, and supplication, prayer filled with words addressed to God in the heart and mind. A number of years later Main read Augustine Baker's *Holy Wisdom* with a young man and was taken by Baker's description of his struggle with the "prayer of acts" and his discovery that the holy hermits early in the Christian tradition had spoken about a form of prayer that was free of images and words.[70] Following in the footsteps of Baker, Main's research led him to John Cassian who, in his Tenth Conference, wrote of this early practice using a single short phrase in the disciplines of stillness (*hesychia*, the Greek word literally meaning "tranquility") that was necessary for prayer: "The mind thus casts out and represses the rich and ample matter of all thoughts and restricts itself to the poverty of a single verse."[71] In reading these words at the heart of early Christian spiritual writing, Main said he arrived "home once more and returned to the practice of the *mantra*."[72]

In his Second Conference Main turned to the purpose of prayer, to the practice of the mantra: liberation. He argued that the danger facing many religious people is that, having stepped onto a pathway of regard for the divine, they take refuge in and surround their spiritual discipline with the prayerful affirmation of propositions about the divine. Prayer becomes a form of anesthesia, a floating piety, or as John Cassian termed it, a *pax perniciosa* (ruinous peace) and a *sopor letalis* (lethal sleep).[73] Prayer that rests in proposition statements of faith, in reaffirming a presumed privileged relationship in the divine scheme of things, in self-complacency and the repetition of creedal formulas, prayer that talks of liberty and solidarity is prayer that does little to open one to be simply present to life. Jesus said that one must lose one's life in order to find it (Matthew 10:39), that a thoroughgoing renunciation was at the heart of the recovery of a whole life, thus, "In the vision of prayer of John Cassian, restricting our mind to one word is proof of the genuineness of our renunciation. In his vision of prayer we renounce thought, imagination, even self-consciousness itself; the matrix of language and reflection."[74]

The mantra is a form of *askesis,* that lovely Greek word from which we get both the word *athlete* and another word for monk, *ascetic.* Just as athletes must discipline their life, let go of many things, both mental and physical, and shape their time and space in service to their goal, so the life of prayer is first a practice in letting go in order to discover and draw near to who one really is. Mantra is a path for letting go, for putting aside those thoughts, words, and feelings that are constantly reinforcing our image of ourselves so that we may discover, in the words of St. Peter, "the inmost center of our being" (1 Peter 3:4). Contemplative prayer with the mantra, Main argued, liberates us from the limitations and distortions of a spiritual life rooted in propositions and moves us from thinking about God to that which is immeasurably greater: seeking to be with God.

How do we move forward to this state of presence? For John Main the first step forward is to adopt the spirit of poverty. In this we also hear the Indian call to renunciation and life modeled by the sannyasi. John Cassian had also spoken of becoming "grandly poor" through the practice of mantra and that this was a way to recover the richness and glory of God and the fullness of life. The vow of poverty monks make symbolizes a detachment far deeper than mere personal possessions. Cassian's call to restrict oneself in prayer to a single verse, the mantra, was a call to the most basic poverty. The practice of the mantra may lead one away from thinking of one's security as grounded in all the affectations of life and Main, speaking to the monks of Gethsemani Abbey, who knew a good deal about poverty, reminded them that this is not a form of self-rejection, a running away from the struggles of life. Rather, poverty is an initial step toward the experience of "our own personal and infinite capacity to be love. The harmony of the real Self that lies beyond all selfishness, beyond all ego-based activity is so well attested to in the Christian tradition. St Catherine of Genoa put it succinctly: 'My *me* is God. Nor do I know my selfhood save in him'."[75] To come to rest in that deep selfhood is the purpose of meditation. When we surrender, "what we die to is, in the thought of Zen, not the self or the mind but rather that *image* of the self or the mind which we have mistakenly come to identify with that which we are. . . . What we are renouncing in prayer is, essentially, *unreality*."[76] In contemplative prayer, in the exercise of mantra, we

> know the need we have to rejoice in our being at its simplest, where it simply exists with no reason for its existence other than that it gives glory to God who created it, who loves it and who sustains it in being. And it is in prayer that we experience the sheer joy that there is in simple being. Having surrendered everything we have, everything by which we exist or know that we exist, we stand before the Lord God in utter simplicity. And the poverty of the single verse that John Cassian enjoins is the means in mediation of losing our life that we may find it, of becoming nothing that we may become the All.[77]

Mantra in Christian North America

A renaissance of contemplative prayer has taken place in the Western Christian Church through the encounter of Monchanin, Le Sault, Griffiths, and Main with the masters of mantra in India. Dialogue and practice led them, and those who have learned from them, back to the sources of the Christian tradition on the prayer of the heart. A curious and charming aspect of this encounter in India has been a new opening of dialogue for both Roman Catholics and Protestants with the Christian East's tradition on the prayer of the heart, hesychasm.[78] Initially a form of monastic prayer, the practice centered on the constant recitation of the short Jesus Prayer: "Lord Jesus Christ, Son of God, have mercy upon me." It is this short prayer that led ancients and moderns alike to the stillness in which the fullness of human nature is known through the presence of God. For Western Christians the recovery of mantra has also meant they could reclaim, as vividly portrayed in the life of John Main, the golden strand of the Christian teaching about silence and the journey to union with God.

The Benedictine Priory of Montreal gave birth to a lay community, the Meditatio Christian Meditation Community. Through the work of John Main, and those who learned from him, national, regional, and local organizations have grown throughout North America and spread through Europe to Asia and Australia. A large body of publications and seminars in local parishes, as well as occasions for those to come, much as John Main himself did, to inquire about the art of prayer, the pathways of peace, and the liberation to be found at the "still point of the turning world" pepper North America. Members of Christian Meditation communities gather Christians and other seekers in the daily discipline through which mantra may lead to stillness and the life of loving kindness.

The chant, which initially brought the singer's inner clamor to the surface, leads to a "recollection" of the self, free from undue attachments. This recollection or recovery occurs in the balance between singing the sacred text and contemplating the sound and silence of the song and music. As Bhartrhari puts it in the *Vakyapadiya.*

> After taking his stand on the word which lies beyond the activity of breath, after having taken rest in oneself by the union resulting in the suppression of sequence, after having purified speech and after having rested it on the mind, after having broken its bonds and made it bond-free, after having reached the inner light, he with his knots cut, becomes united with the Supreme Light.[79]

CONCLUSION: AN OVERVIEW

We began this study with an arrival in India amid both the noise of the city and the quiet chant of prayers to greet the dawn. Beginning with the Rgveda experience of mantra as revealed word, we surveyed the ritual function of mantras in the Brahmanas and the meditation on mantras such as *tat tvam asi* in the Upanisads as a prescription for moksa or release. The crucial role played by mantras in each of the four stages of life was examined, as was the ritual use of mantras in homes and temples. We saw that just as the day begins with mantra chanting, so also it closes with an evening prayer. Just as one is named after birth, initiated, married, and given diksa by mantra, so also one dies and is placed on the funeral pyre in mantra. Even the sounds of nature, from the song of birds to the roar of waves, speak forth the mantra of the universe to one who listens.

But to listen so that one really hears requires the removal of karmic obstructions from our consciousness—obstructions that have built up from actions and thoughts in this and previous lifetimes, backward infinitely. We saw how various schools developed both theories and practical disciplines for the removal of karma from consciousness, employing mantra chanting in a variety of yogas or spiritual disciplines. The approaches offered by the Mimamsa, Grammarian, Yogic, and Tantric schools all claimed the ability to use mantras in such a way that enlightenment and release from karma-samsara, birth, death, and rebirth, would be realized.

On the question of how to find one's own mantra we examined the need for a guru to prescribe the mantra particularly suited to the devotee's particular karma. We observed that for the masses of Hindus it is often mantra in the form of sermons by a traveling preacher or vyasa that provides their central devotional experience. The bhakti or devotional singing of mantras as hymns or kirtans—a practice common to both Hindus and Sikhs—is common as well. In an equally powerful but more esoteric vein there is the Tibetan Buddhist chanting (with ritual gestures and roles) of OM MANI PADME HUM in the D-major chord. Mantra singing is claimed by all of these traditions to be an effective way to release or enlightenment.

FIGURE 3.10 Western meditators at the Ganges, Banaras. COURTESY RONALD NEUFELDT

Although our focus has been mainly on Hindu mantra practice as a means for hearing the divine, we have included examples from other religions wherever possible. Thus, among the religions present in India we have noted Sikh, Sufi, Tibetan Buddhist, and Christian use of mantras. All of these need to be taken together for the full flavor of mantra as a hearing of the divine. From time to time we have also discussed Western experiences or religious practices that in some sense might be functionally parallel to the Indian use of mantra. We also examined some of the forms mantra use has taken on in North America.

Glossary

acarya Teacher, spiritual guide, in traditional Indian education used as equivalent to an MA degree.

Agni Fire; Vedic god of fire, light, and truth; symbolically the fire that comes to light the dawn each morning.

amrit The Sikh initiation or baptism ceremony in which a personal mantra is received from the scripture, the Guru Granth Sahib.

anadi The Indian notion that there is no absolute creation, that everything has always been going on beginninglessly.

artha The pursuit of the wealth needed to fulfill the householder obligations of providing for one's family and supporting others in the community, especially the forest or *asrama* dwellers and *sannyasis* or holy wanderers.

asana Sitting posture or pose for meditation, e.g., the lotus pose with the legs crossed and heels on thighs.

asrama A stage of life (there are four in the Indian tradition); a hermitage.

bhajana Devotional recitation.

bhakti Devotion; love of God.

bija-mantra A "seed sound" that supports and calls into being a particular god or level of consciousness. By repeating a bija-mantra correctly the devotee is said to appropriate its ontological essence.

bodhisattva An enlightened one who will become a Buddha but who turns back to help all those still trapped in suffering and ignorance.

Brahman The absolute, the divine for Hinduism; sometimes characterized as pure consciousness.

Brahmana A prose commentary on the original Vedic mantras composed by the brahmin priests for mainly ritual purposes.

brahmin The priestly class or a member of the priestly class, charged with the duties of learning, teaching, and performing rituals.

cakra "Centers," located between the base of the spine and the top of the head; that refer not to ordinary bodily organs but to the Tantric theory of subtle bodies or centers up and down the spine that correlate with cosmic powers and must be awakened by meditation. Each center has its own mantra and visual symbol (see figure 2.3).

daivi vak The divine word that descends and embodies itself in the words of language, especially the sacred words of scripture and mantra. Somewhat parallel to the Western notion of logos as used in John 1:1.

darshan The "auspicious sight" of the deity; involves both a seeing and being seen by the divine image. Also a philosophical position, a point of view or a way of seeing the universe.

dharana Meditation by keeping the mind concentrated on a single point. In the case of mantra meditation the mantra is the single-point of concentration.

dharani Mutilated words (e.g., *amale, vimale, hime,* etc., that express ideas of purity) or unintelligible syllables (e.g. *hrim, hram, hrum, phat,* etc.), which, like mantras, are chanted as "supports" or aids to meditation in Tantric practice. To the initiated these sounds reveal their meaning during meditation.

dharma One's religious and moral duty in life; doing one's dharma produces spiritual merit; may also mean truth.

diksa The initiation ceremony of a devotee by a guru—the key part being the whispering of the mantra specially selected by the guru for the devotee into the devotee's ear.

garbhagrha The "womb chamber" or center of a Hindu temple where the image of the deity is found.

Gayatri mantra Is given as a part of the Vedic sacred thread (*upanayana*) ceremony. The mantra is addressed to the old Rgvedic solar god Savit.

gurbani God's word spoken by the guru in Sikhism.

gurdwara A Sikh temple.

guru Teacher, spiritual director; sometimes seen as a channel through which the divine may flow to the devotee; prescriber of mantra suited to the spiritual or karmic condition of the devotee.

Guru Granth Sahib The Sikh scripture composed of the hymns of the Sikh gurus, collected by Arjun and finalized by Gobind Singh, who designated it as *the living guru.* It is judged to be God's words spoken through Nanak and the other gurus. Also called the Adi Granth.

Isvara In the view of the Yoga school, the divine guru of the ancient rsis; it is the divine word of the Veda in its transcendental essence that makes up the pure consciousness of *Isvara.*

Isvarapranidhanam Offering up of all action and thought to *Isvara.*

japa The repetition of a mantra or the name of God.

karma The trace or seed left behind by each thought or action that predisposes one to a similar thought or action in the future (as defined in Patanjali's *Yoga Sutras*); a cause of *samsara* or rebirth.

katha Oral preaching in storytelling style of the Hindu text the *Ramayana* by specially trained scholars (*vyasas*).

Khalsa The Sikh term for the holy congregation of those initiated through the ceremony of *amrit.*

kirtan Singing hymns of praise as a part of devotion (*bhakti*).

kratu An energy within the word that seeks to burst forth into expression; the drive to diversity within the unitary divine word (*Sabdabrahman*).

krpa Compassion; divine mercy.

Kundalini In Tantrism, the symbolization of the Great Goddess, *Sakti*, "energy" in the form of a snake that is in a sleeping coil at the base of the spine. When awakened by the initiation and guidance of a guru, it rises through the cakras or centers along the spine with the aid of meditation and mantra chanting. Some texts see this process as the transmutation of sexual energy into spiritual energy.

logos (Greek), word, reason; in Christian doctrine the Second Person of the Trinity; used in a mystical sense by Neo-Platonist philosophers and in the Gospel of John, chapter 1.

Mahayana One of the main schools or traditions of Buddhism.

Mahesvara Lord.

mandala A circular diagram that functions as a symbolic map of the universe. Temples, cities, and paintings use it as a basic form. The Western psychologist Carl Jung used it as a model of the various levels of consciousness within the personality.

mantra Word, formula verse (especially from scriptures), or sound believed to have magical, religious, or spiritual power when recited, muttered, sung, or meditated upon.

moksa (**karma-samsara**) Liberation, release from the beginningless cycle of birth-death-rebirth.

murti Form of likeness; the image of the deity used as a focus for worship and *darshan.*

Nam The seed sound or mantra for Sikhs; meditation upon it leads to union with God and release from the *samsara* cycle of the birth, death, and rebirth.

pasyanti The level of intuitive or flashlike understanding of the meaning-whole (*sphoa*).

prakrti Matter, nature; a technical term in the Sankhya and yoga schools particularly; composed of the three constituent qualities or *gunas*; *sattva* (transparency), *rajas* (movement, passion), and *tamas* (inertia).

prana Breath.

pranayama Control of respiration; in mantra practice it involves breathing in a specified way with the chanting, e.g., in chanting *hamsa* the breath is inhaled with *ham* and expelled with *sa.*

prasad "Favor, grace." In worship, the food that is offered to the deity and then returned, consecrated, as the "grace" of the Lord to the devotee; also consecrated food given to the devotee by the guru during the *diksa* or initiation ritual.

puja "Worship." Usually involves the presentation of offerings to the deity.

purusa Self or soul in the Sankhya or yoga schools; individual to each person; pure consciousness.

Qur'an The Islamic scripture; the word of Allah as spoken to Muhammad through the angel Gabriel.

raga In Indian music a basic tune or melody.

Rama Lila A play or folk drama of the Hindu epic poem the *Ramayana.*

Rgveda One of India's Hindu scriptures; a part of *sruti*; a collection of ancient mantras "heard" or "seen" by the rsis.

rsi An original "hearer" or "seer" of the Hindu mantras at the start of each creation cycle. One who has purged oneself of all karmic obscuration (ignorance), rendering consciousness transparent to the divine word.

rta The Vedic principle of moral truth and order, immanent in both the cosmos and the individual.

sabda Word, testimony of a trustworthy person; word or words that when spoken convey knowledge—especially of the divine.

Sabdabraham The absolute, the divine for Bharthari and the Grammarians; the intertwined unity of word and consciousness that is the one ultimate reality; also called the divine word or *daivi vak.*

Sakti Power, potency, in Tantrism the Great Goddess or Divine Mother raised to the level of a cosmic force that sustains the whole universe and its many manifestations of gods. At the human level it incarnates in woman who symbolizes both the mystery of creation and the power of being.

samadhi Trance state of consciousness with no subject-object separation.

samsara Rebirth in the suffering and bondage of this world; the continual round of birth-death-rebirth from which release is eventually desired.

samskaras Rites, "sacraments"; e.g., the "sacred thread" vedic initiation ceremony (*Upanayana*) of the young boy of the three upper castes.

sannyasin Renouncer, one who has given up attachment to material possessions, sensuous pleasures, family, and caste attachments for a life of contemplation, wandering, and asceticism—the fourth stage of life from which *moksa* or release may be realized.

smrti Secondary Hindu scripture (from an orthodox Brahmanical perspective); that which has been remembered, e.g., the *Bhagavad Gita* or the *Ramayana*; contrasts with *sruti.*

sphota A meaning-whole or idea that eternally exists within consciousness and is evoked or manifested by the speaking of mantras; can be directly perceived through intuition.

sruti Primary Hindu scripture; that which has been directly heard and seen by the *rsis* or seers; includes the Vedic mantras, Brahmanas, and Upanisads. Contrasted with *smrti.*

Sufism A mystical tradition of Islam frequently found in India. It emphasizes the mystical or intuitive approach to the Qur'an.

svadhyaya Concentrated meditative study and chanting of mantra verses and the syllable OM.

tika Subcommentary or gloss on a main commentary.

Upanayana Vedic initiation ceremony of the young boy with sacred thread and Gayatri mantra.

Upanisad The last portion of the Vedas, a prose commentary composed by a guru usually in teacher-student dialogue. The goal is the student's inner realization of the truth of the Vedic teaching.

vak Language or speech, thought of as having various levels from the gross form of the spoken word to the subtle form of the highest intuition.

vak lao The Sikh process of opening the scripture, the Guru Granth Sahib, at random and reading from the first verse on the top left page. God is understood to be selecting the passage.

vakya Sentence; sentence meaning.

vasana A habit pattern of thought and/or action composed of reinforced or repeated karmic patterns or *samskaras.*

Vedas The primary Hindu scriptures including the early hymns or mantras, the Brahmanas and Upanisads. The Vedas are organized into four collections called Rg, Sama, Yajur, and Atharva.

Wahiguru Sikh mantra that proclaims God as guru. In this mantra sounds the essential vibration of the eternal absolute, where the one God is said to reside. Chanting it removes ignorance, opening the way to direct communication with God.

yantra A "device" for harnessing the mind in meditation or worship. A diagram, usually of interlocking triangles and circles.

Notes

1. Hearing the Sacred

1. As quoted by Andre Padoux in Harvey P. Alper, ed., *Understanding Mantras* (Albany: State University of New York Press, 1989), p. 296.

2. Diana L. Eck, *Darshan: Seeing the Divine Image in India*, 3d ed. (New York: Columbia University Press, 1998), p. 3.

3. Diana L. Eck, *A New Religious America: How a "Christian Country" Has Become the World's Most Religiously Diverse Nation* (San Francisco: HarperSanFrancisco, 2001), see, e.g., pp. 90–94. See also Rachel Fell McDermott and Jeffrey J. Kripal, eds., *Encountering Kali: In the Margins, at the Center, in the West* (Berkeley: University of California Press, 2003); and Padma Rangaswamy, *Namaste America: Indian Immigrants in an American Metropolis* (University Park: Pennsylvania State University Press, 2000).

4. Swami Agehananda Bharati, *The Ochre Robe* (Garden City, NY: Doubleday, 1970), p. 161.

5. Swami Agehananda Bharati, *The Tantric Tradition* (London: Rider, 1970), p. 102

6. *Yoga Sutras* 2.12–14 and 4.7–9. For an English translation see James Haughton Woods, trans., *The Yoga-System of Pantanjali: or, The Ancient Hindu Doctrine of Concentration of Mind, Embracing the Mnemonic Rules, Called the Yoga-Sutras, of Patanjali*, Harvard Oriental series, vol. 17, 3d ed. (Delhi: Motilal Banarsidass, 1966), hereinafter cited as *Y.-S.* For a detailed analysis of the passages in question see Harold G. Coward, "Psychology and Karma," *Philosophy East and West* 33 (1983): 49–60.

7. See Ellison Banks Findly, "Mantra kavisasta: Speech as Performative in the Rgveda," in Alper, *Understanding Mantras*, p. 15.

8. Rudolf Otto, *The Idea of the Holy: An Inquiry Into the Non-Rational Factor in the Idea of the Divine and Its Relation to the Rational*, John W. Harvey, trans., 2d ed. (New York: Oxford University Press, 1958), pp. 4–7.

9. Jan Gonda, "The Indian *Mantra*," *Oriens* 16 (1963): 247.

10. Aurobindo Ghose, *The Secret of the Veda* (Pondicherry: Sri Aurobindo Ashram, 1956), p. 6.

11. See Thomas B. Coburn, "Scripture in India," *Journal of the American Academy of Religion* 52 (1984): 447.

12. Findly, "Mantra kavisasta," p. 17.

13. Paul Hacker, "Notes on the Mandukyopanisad and Sankara's Agamasastravivarana," in J. Ensink and Hans Peter Theodor Gaeffke, eds., *India Maior: Congratulatory Volume Presented to J. Gonda* (Leiden: Brill, 1972), p. 118.

14. Findly, "Mantra kavisasta," p. 20.

15. Ibid., pp. 21–22.

16. Ibid.

17. Ibid., p. 26.

18. J. L. Austin, "Performative Utterances" in *Philosophical Papers* (Oxford: Oxford University Press, 1961), pp. 220–239.

19. Stanley Jeyaraja Tambiah, *Culture, Thought and Social Action: An Anthropological Perspective* (Cambridge: Harvard University Press, 1985), pp. 17–59.

20. Findly, "Mantra kavisasta," p. 28.

21. Ibid., p. 43.

22. George Weston Briggs, *Gorakhnath and the Kanphata Yogis* (Delhi: Motilal Banarsidass, 1982).

23. A rich description of the Upanayana ritual can be found in Raj Bali Pandey, *Hindu Samskaras: Socio-Religious Study of the Hindu Sacraments* (Delhi: Motilal Banarsidass, 1976).

24. Ibid., p. 131.

25. Ibid., p. 136.

26. Padoux, in Alper, *Understanding Mantras*, p. 311.

27. Rai Bahadur Srira Chandra Vidyarnava, *The Daily Practice of the Hindus, Containing the Morning and Midday Duties*, 4th ed. (New Delhi: Oriental Books Reprint, 1979).

28. *The Great Liberation* (Mahanirvana Tantra), trans., with commentary, Sir John Woodroffe, 5th ed. (Madras: Ganesh, 1971), p. 138.

29. As quoted by W. Owen Cole, *The Guru in Sikhism* (London: Darton, Longman and Todd, 1982), p. 55.

30. See Pashaura Singh, *The Guru Granth Sahib: Canon, Meaning, and Authority* (New York: Oxford University Press, 2000).

31. For a discussion of Sikh ritual practice and meaning of sacred language see David J. Goa and Harold G. Coward, "Ritual, Word, and Meaning in Sikh Religious Life," *Journal of Sikh Studies* 13, no. 2 (August 1986).

2. The Nature of Mantra

1. Frits Staal, "gveda 10.71 on the Origin of Language," in Harold G. Coward and

Krishna Sivaraman, eds., *Revelation in Indian Thought: A Festschrift in Honour of Professor T. R. V. Murti* (Emeryville, CA: Dharma, 1977), pp. 5–6.

2. As quoted by T. R. V. Murti in "Foreword" to Harold G. Coward, *The Sphota Theory of Language: A Philosophical Analysis* (Delhi: Motilal Banarsidass, 1980), p. viii.

3. See Frits Staal, "Oriental Ideas on the Origin of Language," *Journal of the American Oriental Society* 99 (1979): 9. In chapter 1 we have likened mantras to "speech acts."

4. See Jan Gonda, "The Indian Mantra," *Oriens* 16 (1964): 261–268.

5. Staal, "Oriental Ideas," p. 10.

6. This presentation of the Mimamsa school's position is based on P. T. Raju, *Structural Depths of Indian Thought* (Albany: State University of New York Press, 1985), chapter 2, pp. 40–77.

7. Shashi Bhushan Dasgupta, *Aspects of Indian Religious Thought* (Calcutta: Firma KLM Pvt., 1977), p. 25.

8. Mircea Eliade, *Yoga: Immortality and Freedom*, trans. Willard R. Trask, 2d ed. (Princeton: Princeton University Press, 1969), p. 212.

9. For a detailed and comprehensive presentation of the Grammarian school's position see Harold G. Coward and K. Kunjunni Raja, eds., *The Philosophy of the Grammarians* (Princeton: Princeton University Press, 1990).

10. K. A. Subramania Iyer, trans., *The Vakyapadiya of Bhartrhari* (Poona: Deccan College Postgraduate and Research Institute, 1965), 1.1 and 1.9; hereinafter cited as *Vak.*

11. Ibid., 1.5.

12. Ibid., 1.123.

13. Ibid., 1.1.

14. Ibid., 1.126.

15. Ibid, 1.332.

16. Ibid., 1.124.

17. T. R. V. Murti, "Some Comments on the Philosophy of Language in the Indian Context," *Journal of Indian Philosophy* 2 (1974): 322.

18. *Vak,* 1.51.

19. Ibid., 1.52, *Vrtti.* Bhartrhari's philosophy presented in the next pages previously appeared in Harold G. Coward, "The Meaning and Power of Mantras in Bhartrhari's *Vakyapadiya*," *Studies in Religion* 11.4 (1982): 370–374.

20. *Vak,* 1:23–26 and 122–123.

21. Ibid., 1:84, *Vrtti.*

22. Ibid., 2 in which Bhartrhari establishes the *Vakya-sphota* or sentence-whole over against the view of the Mimamsakas.

23. *Vak,* 1:24–26, *Vrtti.*

24. See Wade Wheelock, "A Taxonomy of the Mantras in the New and Full Moon Sacrifice," *History of Religion* 19 (1980): 358.

25. W. T. Stace, *Mysticism and Philosophy* (London: Macmillan, 1961), p. 15. This is, of

course, exactly the opposite of the common modern interpretations given to the term *mystical,* e.g., vague, mysterious, and foggy.

26. *Vak,* 1:142. Note that in *Vrtti* sounds of cart axle, drum, and flute are all forms of manifested Vak, and therefore potentially meaningful mantras.

27. Ibid., 1:152–154.

28. Gonda, "The Indian Mantra," p. 271.

29. *Vak,* 1:89.

30. For a more complete analysis see Harold G. Coward, "The Yoga of the Word (Sabdapurvayoga)," *Adyar Library Bulletin* 49 (1985): 1–13.

31. For an overview of the Yoga system of Patanjali and some aspects of Tantrism see Jean Varenne, *Yoga and the Hindu Tradition,* trans. Derek Coltman (Delhi: Motilal Banarsidass, 1989).

32. For an English translation see *Y.-S.*

33. *Y.-S.,* 1:24–29.

34. Ibid., 1.5.

35. Ibid., 2.44.

36. *Bhasya* or Commentary on *Y.-S.,* 1:28 as rendered in *Patanjali's Yoga Sutras: With the Commentary of Vyasa and the Gloss of Vachaspati Misra,* trans. Rama Prasada, reprint of 2d ed. (New Delhi: Oriental, 1978), p. 51.

37. In making these parallel comparisons between Patanjali's Yoga and Bhartrhari's Grammarian philosophy, a technical qualification must be entered. It must be realized that at the highest level of basic presuppositions, there are fundamental differences between the two philosophies. Bhartrhari offers an absolutism of word-consciousness or Sabdabrahman while the Yoga system is ultimately a duality between pure consciousness (*purusa*) and nonintelligent matter (*prakrti*). Consequently, Isvara's *sattva* (transparent mind) as itself a part of prakrti does not have the power of consciousness (*Y.-S.,* 1:24, *Tika*). Since our concern here is not with the ultimate nature of the metaphysics involved, the discussion has proceeded as if the sattva aspect of prakrti were indeed real consciousness. This is in accord with the yoga view of the nature of the psychological processes. The sattva aspect of *citta,* insofar as it is clear, takes on or reflects the intelligence (*caitanya*) of purusa. For practical purposes, therefore, no duality appears, and prakrti may be treated as self-illuminating (see *Tika* on *Y.-S.,* 1:17).

38. *Y.-S.,* 2:45.

39. Gerhard Oberhammer makes this claim in his article, "The Use of Mantra in Yogic Meditation: The Testimony of the *Pasupata,*" in Harvey P. Alper, ed., *Understanding Mantras* (Albany: State University of New York Press, 1989), p. 204. Oberhammer takes pains to make clear, however, that theistic mantra meditation followed by the *Pasupata* is fundamentally different from that of Patanjali's yoga in that it aims at a union of the soul or self (*atma*) of the devotee with the Lord (the *Mahesvara*). For Patanjali there is no real union of the devotee's purusa with that of Isvara. Rather Isvara is simply a perfect purusa or self that the devotee through mantra samadhi can attempt to emulate in his or her individual yogic practice.

40. Ibid., p. 219.

41. Eliade, *Yoga*, p. 200.

42. Wheelock, "Mantra in Vedic and Tantric Ritual," in Alper, ed. *Understanding Mantras*, p. 117.

43. Eliade, *Yoga*, p. 202. Most scholars seem to agree with Eliade that the goddess impulse of Tantrism may be traced to the Dravidian culture of South India. The tradition further suggests that this need to switch from male to female dominance is occasioned by the general increase in impurity as the cycle of creation enters its final phase, the *kaliyuga*. Only the Sakti or Great Goddess has sufficient power to deal with this increase in impurity (Eliade, *Yoga*, p. 203).

44. Ibid., pp. 202–205.

45. Ibid., p. 212.

46. Ibid., p. 213. The following sentences are based on Eliade, *Yoga*, p. 214.

47. Ibid., p. 215. For the traditional view and three modern theories regarding bija-mantras see Swami Agehananda Bharati, *The Tantric Tradition* (London: Rider, 1970), pp. 115–119, from which the following description of bija-mantras is taken.

48. Ibid., p. 242.

49. Ibid., p. 215.

50. Ibid., p. 216. Eliade gives the example of Vasubandhu, who in his *Bodhisattvabhumi* says that the true meaning of the mantras is found in their absence of meaning. In modern scholarship Frits Staal maintains this position. See his "Sanskrit Philosophy of Language," *Current Trends in Linguistics* 5 (1969): 463–497.

51. Harvey P. Alper, "The Cosmos as Siva's Language-Game" in Alper, ed., *Understanding Mantras*, p. 268.

3. Finding One's Mantra

1. Harvey P. Alper, "The Cosmos as Siva's Language Game,"in Harvey P. Alper, ed., *Understanding Mantras* (Albany: State University of New York Press, 1989), p. 258.

2. Ibid., p. 262.

3. See Swami Agehananda Bharati, *The Tantric Tradition* (London: Rider, 1970). On pp. 119 and 120 the author offers examples of such "disguised" Hindu and Buddhist mantra texts.

4. Ibid. Bharati offers several pages of translation from the Hindi text on pp. 123–128.

5. As translated by Alper in "The Cosmos as Siva's Language Game," p. 249.

6. Ibid., p. 263, as translated by Alper.

7. Ibid., verse 76, as translated by Alper.

8. Ibid., p. 281, Ksemaraja's commentary on verse 113, as translated by Alper.

9. Ibid., p. 282, as translated by Alper.

10. Bharati, *The Tantric Tradition*, p. 185.

11. Ibid., p. 186.

12. Ibid., p. 187.

13. Ibid., p. 189. This summary is based on Bharati, *The Tantric Tradition*, pp. 188–189.

14. For a detailed discussion of the more equal position of girls in the early Vedic period see Harold G. Coward, Julius Lipner, and Katherine K. Young, *Hindu Ethics: Purity, Abortion, and Euthanasia* (Albany: State University of New York Press, 1989), pp. 13–14.

15. Diana L. Eck, *A New Religious America: How a "Christian Country" Has Become the World's Most Religiously Diverse Nation* (San Francisco: HarperSanFrancisco, 2001), p. 109.

16. Ibid., pp. 110–111.

17. Ibid., p. 117.

18. Ibid., p. 119.

19. The following is based on Phillip Lutgendorf, "The Life of a Text: Tulsidasa's *Ramacaritamansa* in Oral Exposition," paper presented at the American Academy of Religion Annual Meeting, Chicago, December, 1984.

20. Ibid., p. 7.

21. Ibid., p. 11.

22. The following summary is based on Gerhard Böwering, "The Islamic Case: A Sufi Vision of Experience" in Peter L. Berger, ed., *The Other Side of God: A Polarity in World Religions* (Garden City, NY: Anchor/Doubleday, 1981); pp. 134–136.

23. Ibid., p. 134.

24. Ibid.

25. Ibid., p. 135.

26. Eck, *A New Religious America*, p. 265.

27. The order was founded by Muin ad-Din Muhammad Chishti (1142–1236) and is prominent in India and Pakistan.

28. While a thorough history of this chapter in the religious life of North America has yet to be written, Jay Kinney's article, "Sufism Comes to America," *Gnosis* (Winter 1994): 18–23, has chronicled the key events.

29. Nirtan Carol Sokoloff in the introduction to Hidayat Inayat Khan, *Sufi Teachings: Lectures from Lake O'Hara* (Victoria, BC: Ekstasis, 1994), p. 8.

30. Hidayat Inayat Khan, *Path of Remembrance: Teachings on the Singing Zikar of Hazrat Inayat Khan* (Groningen: Sufi Centre Groningen, International Sufi Movement, 1999).

31. Ibid., p. 28.

32. Najim al-Din Razi, *The Path of God's Bondsmen from Origin to Return: A Sufi Compendium*, ed. and trans. Hamid Algar (Delmar, NY: Caravan, 1982), p. 270.

33. *Mathnavi* 5, vv. 588–590.

34. Inayat Khan, *Path of Remembrance*, p. 9.

35. Ibid., p. 13.

36. Ibid.

37. Quoted in Farid al-Din 'Attar, *Muslim Saints and Mystics: Episodes from the Tadhkirat al-Auliya'*, trans. A. J. Arberry (Chicago: University of Chicago Press, 1966), p. 51.

38. Ibid., p. 43.

39. Kirpal Singh Khalsa, "New Religious Movements Turn to Worldly Success," *Journal for the Scientific Study of Religion* 25.2 (June 1986): 233–247.

40. Yogi Bhajan, *Kri Pilot Manual*, 2002, as noted on the 3HO Web site.

41. Yogi Bhajan, *The Teachings of Yogi Bhajan* (New York: Hawthorn, 1977), p. ix.

42. Ibid., p. 14.

43. Ibid., p. 85.

44. Ibid., p. 89.

45. This section is based on Joseph T. O'Connell, "Caitanya's Followers and *Bhagavad Gita*: A Case Study in *Bhakti* and the Secular," pp. 33–52, and Norvin J. Hein, "Caitanya's Ecstasies and the Theology of the Name," pp. 15–32, both in Bardwell L. Smith, ed., *Hinduism: New Essays in the History of Religions* (Leiden: Brill, 1976).

46. W. G. Archer, *The Loves of Krishna in Indian Painting and Poetry* (New York: Macmillan, 1957), p. 79.

47. Interview with Kiran Gill, Calgary, Alberta, Canada, April 14, 1985.

48. Interview with Dr. Ranjit Dhaliwal, Calgary, Alberta, Canada, February 15, 1985.

49. This is a very complex matter, and we have only touched on its meaning and practice. It has been considered at length in the classic study by Giuseppe Tucci, *The Religions of Tibet*, trans. Geoffrey Samuel (Berkeley: University of California Press, 1980) and in Robert Brainerd Ekvall's *Religious Observances in Tibet: Patterns and Function* (Chicago: University of Chicago Press, 1964). This phenomenon is well presented in Huston Smith's film of Tibetan Buddhism, *Requiem for a Faith*, filmed in northern India.

50. Rembert Herbert, "Singer, Text, and Song," *Parabola* 14.4 (1989): 17–23.

51. Ibid., p. 20.

52. Ibid.

53. The history of this early chapter in Christian India is explored in Stephen Neill, *A History of Christianity in India: The Beginnings to A.D. 1707* (New York: Cambridge University Press, 1984) and Samuel Hugh Moffett, *A History of Christianity in Asia: Beginnings to 1500*, 2d rev. ed. (Maryknoll, NY: Orbis, 1998).

54. Jules Monchanin, *In Quest of the Absolute: The Life and Work of Jules Monchanin*, trans. and ed. Joseph G. Weber (Kalamazoo, MI: Cistercian, 1977).

55. Swami Abhishiktananda, *Saccidananda: A Christian Approach to Advaitic Experience* (Delhi: I.S.P.C.K-L.P.H., 1974) first appeared as *Sagesse hindoue mystique chrétienne du védanta à la Trinité* (Paris: Centurion, 1965).

56. For a thorough discussion of the process leading to the document *Nostra Aetate* see volume 3 of *Commentary on the Documents of Vatican II*, Herbert Vorgrimler, general editor (Freiburg/Montreal: Herder/Palm, 1968), pp. 1–154. Analysis of the history of the text is followed by illuminating essays: Cyril B. Papali, "Excursus on Hinduism" and Heinrich Dumoulin, "Excursus on Buddhism."

57. Wayne Teasdale, "Bede Griffiths," in William M. Johnston, ed., *Encyclopedia of Monasticism* (Chicago: Fitzroy Dearborn, 2000), p. 555.

58. Emmanuel Mounier (1905–1950), editor of the influential journal *Esprit*, had argued that human nature is "wholly body and wholly spirit," that each person is unique and irreplaceable and subjecting anyone to collective identity alone is illusory, and that the "relation of the person to Nature is not purely exterior but a dialectic of exchange and ascensions." See his books *Be Not Afraid: Studies in Personalist Sociology*, trans. Cynthia Rowland (London: Rockliff, 1951), *Personalism*, trans. Philip Mairet (London: Routledge and Paul, 1952), "Personnalisme et Christianisme" (1946), and his *Manifeste au service du Personnalisme* (Paris: Aubier, 1936), translated by Monks of St. John's Abbey as *A Personalist Manifesto* (London: Longmans, 1938).

59. Teasdale, "Bede Griffiths," p. 555.

60. The writings of John Main of particular interest to us are *Christian Meditation: The Gethsemani Talks*, 2d ed. (Montreal: Benedictine Priory of Montreal, 1982), a series of three talks he gave in November 1976 to the Cistercian community of Gethsemani Abbey, which was home to the well-known monk Thomas Merton; *Christian Meditation, Prayer in the Tradition of John Cassian: Three Conferences* (Montreal: Benedictine Priory of Montreal, 1977); *Monastic Prayer and Modern Man* (Montreal: Benedictine Priory of Montreal, 1983); *Community of Love* (Montreal: Benedictine Priory of Montreal, 1983); and *Word into Silence* (New York: Paulist, 1981). See also Neil McKenty, *In the Stillness Dancing: The Journey of John Main* (London: Darton, Longman and Todd, 1986).

61. Swami Satyananda had, like the Benedictine monk Henri Le Saux, studied with the modern Indian master Ramana Maharshi.

62. Augustine Baker, *Holy Wisdom or Directions for the Prayer of Contemplation* (Wheathampstead: Anthony Clarke, 1972).

63. The two major works by John Cassian (c. 360–after 430) have recently been published in a fine English translation by Boniface Ramsey, OP: *John Cassian: The Conferences* (New York: Paulist, 1997) and *John Cassian: The Institutes* (New York: Newman, 2000), both in the Ancient Christian Writers series.

64. In the organization's newsletter, *Christian Meditation in Canada*, and on their Web site, www. wccm.org, one may quickly glimpse the broad international work of this center to cultivate contemplative prayer and meditation.

65. Gethsemani Abbey in Kentucky was the home of the well-known and prolific monk, Thomas Merton, who died in December 1968 at a conference in Bangkok, where Benedictines from around the world had gathered in dialogue on the spiritual treasures of the East with those inside and outside their tradition. A year after his death the Cistercians published *The Climate of Monastic Prayer* (Spencer, MA: Cistercian, 1969), a series of essays Merton wrote for the monastic community. This book is a classic in the renaissance of contemplative prayer. The proceedings of the Bangkok conference mark a watershed in this renaissance and was edited by John Moffitt and published under the title *A New Charter for Monasticism: Proceedings of the Meeting of the Monastic Superiors in the Far East, Bangkok, December 9 to 15, 1968* (Notre Dame, IN: University of Notre Dame Press, 1970) and is dedicated to Fr. Louis, or Thomas Merton, as he is known to the world.

66. This method of prayer was developed by St. Ignatius of Loyola (1491–1556) in his highly influential book, *Spiritual Exercises.* It stands squarely in the *kataphatikic,* affirmative tradition of Christian spiritual practice, while the monks discussed are on a pathway to the recovery of the *apophatic* tradition associated with the holy men and women of the desert during the early Christian Church.

67. Main, *Christian Meditation: Prayer in the Tradition,* p. 3. These talks were also published in three consecutive issues of *Cistercian Studies,* 1977–1978.

68. Ibid., p. 3.

69. Ibid., p. 4.

70. These struggles are discussed in the four-volume body of texts of these hermits, *The Philokalia: The Complete Text, compiled by St. Nikodimos of the Holy Mountain and St. Makarios of Corinth,* trans. and eds. G. E. H. Palmer, Philip Sherrard, and Kallistos Ware (London: Faber and Faber, 1979–1995).

71. Main, *Christian Meditation: Prayer in the Tradition,* p. 5.

72. Ibid.

73. Ibid., p. 15.

74. Ibid.

75. Ibid., p. 14.

76. Ibid.

77. Ibid., p. 5.

78. Central to the tradition of the prayer of the heart is the work of Gregory of Palamas, theologian, archbishop of Thessalonike (1347–1359), and saint. His teaching on the prayer of the heart, the art of emptying oneself and coming to stillness and union with God, is contained in his *The Triads,* ed. John Meyendorff, trans. Nicholas Gendle (New York: Paulist, 1983).

79. *The Vakyapadiya of Bhartrhari,* trans. K. A. Subramania Iyer (Poona: Deccan College Postgraduate and Research Institute, 1965), 1.131, *Vrtti,* p. 119.

Bibliography

General

Basham, A. L. *The Wonder That Was India: A Survey of the Culture of the Indian Subcontinent Before the Coming of the Muslims.* New York: Grove, 1959. A good survey of the classical context of Indian religion before the coming of the Muslims.

Baird, Robert D., ed. *Religion in Modern India.* 3d ed. New Delhi: Manohar, 1995. A good survey of religious movements and thinkers in modern India.

Coward, Harold G. *Scripture in the World Religions: A Short Introduction.* Oxford: Oneworld, 2000. A comparative study of the role of oral and written word in the religious experience of Judaism, Christianity, Islam, Hinduism, Sikhism, and Buddhism. A new edition of *Sacred Word and Sacred Text: Scripture in World Religions.*

Eck, Diana L. *Darshan: Seeing the Divine Images in India.* 3d ed. New York: Columbia University Press, 1998. An excellent introduction to Hinduism in terms of seeing the divine through sacred images. A companion to this volume.

Eck, Diana L. *A New Religious America: How a "Christian Country" Has Become the World's Most Religiously Diverse Nation.* San Francisco: HarperSanFrancisco, 2001. A survey of how Hindus and other immigrants have brought their religious practices to America and the adaptations that have taken place.

Klostermaier, Klaus K. *A Survey of Hinduism.* 2d ed. Albany: State University of New York Press, 1994. An excellent comprehensive introduction to Hinduism with a much fuller treatment of the bhakti traditions than is usually found.

Koller, John M. *The Indian Way.* New York: Macmillan, 1982. A comprehensive survey of Indian religion with a philosophical emphasis. Includes Hinduism, Jainism, Buddhism, Islam, and Sikhism and is sensitive to the traditional perspective.

The Nature and Use of Mantra

Alper, Harvey, ed.. *Understanding Mantras.* Albany: State University of New York Press, 1989. Certainly the most thorough set of studies on mantra in English. These studies by leading authors in the field explore the meaning and use of mantra in the major Hindu schools of thought and in various historical periods. The editor has provided a definitive bibliography on the subject as well.

Bharati, Swami Agehanánda. *The Tantric Tradition.* London: Rider, 1970. This study includes a consideration of the philosophical content of tantra with an excellent chapter on mantra. Mantra is also central to the author's analysis of Tantric ritual and meditation practice.

Coward, Harold G. *Bhartrhari.* Boston: Twayne, 1976. The great Indian thinker's contribution to Indian philosophy of language with its implications for the understanding of mantra is placed in the context of human psychology and aesthetics in this study.

Coward, Harold. G., and K. Kunjunni Raja, eds. *The Philosophy of the Grammarians.* Princeton: Princeton University Press, 1990. A comprehensive study of classical Indian Grammarian philosophy and the basis it provides for mantra as a means to realizing moksa or release.

Eliade, Mircea. *Yoga: Immortality and Freedom.* Trans. Willard R. Trask. 2d ed. Princeton: Princeton University Press, 1969. Although a somewhat older study, Eliade's consideration of the Yoga and Tantric traditions and the place of mantra within them remains reliable and insightful.

Gonda, Jan. "The Indian Mantra." *Oriens* 16 (1963): 244–297. This essay stands as a classic study of the subject and continues to be well worth reading.

Gunindar Kaur. *The Guru Granth Sahib: Its Physics and Metaphysics.* New Delhi: Sterling, 1981. There are few studies of the Sikh understanding of mantra. This book examines the Sikh understanding of the mantric character of Sikh scripture.

Mantra in Christianity

Trapnell, Judson B. *Bede Griffiths: A Life in Dialogue.* Albany: State University of New York Press, 2001.

Index